C000152261

A Month-by-Month Guide
to
Entertaining Angels

Do not neglect to show hospitality to strangers, for by doing
that some have entertained angels without knowing it.

Hebrews 13:2

The icon on the front cover is by contemporary artist Emil Stoenescu based on the original by Andrei Rublev, a Russian iconographer of the 15th century. Known as "Old Testament Trinity" or "The Hospitality of Abraham," this famous icon is based on the story of the LORD's visit accompanied by two angels to Abraham and Sarah by the oak of Mamre (Genesis 18). It depicts the three angelic visitors seated at table, with Abraham and Sarah in the background.

A MONTH
BY MONTH
GUIDE TO

ENTERTAINING

ANGELS

Mark G. Boyer

Foreword by John Shea

ACTA
ASSISTING CHRISTIANS TO ACT
PUBLICATIONS

A Month-by-Month Guide to Entertaining Angels
by Mark G. Boyer

Edited by LaVonne Neff
Cover art by Emil Stoenescu
Design by Tom A. Wright
Typesetting by Garrison Publications

The Scripture quotations contained herein are from the New Revised Standard Version Bible: Catholic Edition, copyright 1993 and 1989 by the Division of Christian Education of the National Council of the Churches of Christ in the U.S.A. Used by permission. All rights reserved.

Copyright © 1995 by Mark G. Boyer

All rights reserved. No part of this publication may be reproduced or transmitted in any form or by any means, electronic or mechanical, or by any information storage and retrieval system, without permission in writing from the publisher:
ACTA Publications (Assisting Christians to Act),
4848 N. Clark Street, Chicago, IL 60640; 312-271-1030.

Year 00 99 98 97 96 95

Printing 7 6 5 4 3 2 1

ISBN 0-87946-121-7

Library of Congress Number: 95-078803

Printed in the United States of America

Contents

Dedicated to

Father James L. Reynolds,

friend, messenger, fellow traveler,

"angel" in disguise

Angels We Have Heard on Low

A Foreword by John Shea

A recent novel begins with a spaceship surging into outer space. One of the astronauts glances out the "portal" at the vast empty expanse. An angel wings by.

It is a marvelous image—an encounter between angel and spaceship. We smile a little. The last thing we expect outside a spaceship is an angel. If the astronaut saw an alien, there would be no problem. Has not *Star Trek, Close Encounters of the Third Kind,* and *E.T.* prepared us for this possibility?

But an angel? For this we are somehow not prepared. Has the human race finally stumbled upon the heavenly courts where winged creatures flit to and fro, alternately praising the Lord and gossiping about the affairs of earth?

If that is so, I am sure my grandfather would feel pleased.

In the late 1950's the first Russian cosmonaut, Yuri Gagarin, soared into space. When he returned to earth, that staunch atheist could not help but boast that he had been to the heavens and found them empty. Neither God nor angels were anywhere to be found.

My grandfather was not happy. Since I was a seminarian at the time, he asked me what I thought of this "shot at the deity." I had just read Paul Tillich on symbolic language, and so I treated my grandfather to the philosophical view that God was not a divine person who really lived in the sky. "Heavenly" God was an image that signified the divine was transcendent, always more than the finite human mind can encompass.

My grandfather gave me a great look of disgust and spoke the truth that was obvious to him: "That commie didn't fly high enough."

Grandfather would be vindicated to read—even in a novel—that an astronaut finally got high enough to see an angel out the spaceship window.

But perhaps there is another way to interpret this fun image of angel and spaceship. It is not that humankind finally flew high enough to bump into angels, the next level up on the hierarchy of beings. It is that the angel came from Earth, along with the humans, and was traveling skyward, along with the humans. In fact, that is what angels are—companions of human adventure. Wherever people are, angels are not far behind. In fact, as in the novel, they are usually winging a little ahead.

Of course, these angelic companions are sent by God, and that is where their reputation as sky creatures comes from. In the ancient cosmology of a three-tier universe, angels lived in heaven with God and were sent by God to Earth. They were under different instructions depending on the situation. Sometimes they carried important information. At other times they made predictions, issued warnings or conferred blessings. But, always they were reminders of the *immanent* divine presence. And in Biblical and Christian faith this reminder is sorely needed.

The Christian imagination stresses divine transcendence, and that transcendence is often imaged as separation. Our Father lives in heaven and we toil on earth. The question then naturally arises—how does the heavenly God communicate with the earthly creatures? Enter angels. Just when we thought we were on our own, an angel arrives to tell us we are part of a larger plot. Angels help us recognize the intimate, invisible workings of God in our lives.

In other words, angels are not heard on high, they are heard on low. They are the personal manifestations of the earthbound grace of God. Even if the background cosmology of angelic visitations is no longer how we view the space-time continuum, this truth of angels remain: They bring God's providential care into the midst of our comings and goings.

Whenever I take Fr. Boyer's advice and entertain angels, I think of the Gospel perspective, "Are not two sparrows sold for a few pennies? Yet not one is forgotten before God." Christian faith holds that divine providence is particular and universal. Nothing is left out. Everything is considered, and it is considered in its most minute detail. Even cheap sparrows, worth only a few pennies, are not forgotten. How much more you, who are worth more than a whole flock of sparrows!

I think this is what angels are all about. There is a piece of folk wisdom about being tempted by the devil (who is, after all, a fallen angel): "The devil doesn't tempt chopped liver." This saying is meant to console someone in the midst of temptation. In other words, you must be doing something right if the devil has showed up to work on you. So too, angels don't visit chopped liver. You must be someone important if an angel accompanies your life.

That is why, among all the angels, my favorites are those who are characterized as guardians. A number of years ago I wrote a poem to honor guardian angels:

I laugh to remember
how
in the second grade
the nun made us slide over
to make room for a guardian angel.
Since I was fat
and the seat thin,
I oozed over the edge
like a melted cheese sandwich
and was plainly aware
of how close God was.
But I have outgrown that angel,
left him behind
like the sign of the cross
before a free throw
in a basketball game.

Yet
if I could tell a son
only one wisdom,
I might whisper
that he had an angel of his own,
not as a valet
or imaginary playmate,
but as companion—
like Tobit had
on his mission of manhood.
Otherwise
he might forget
his father's mature faith
that the wings of God's love
beat above us all.

I laugh to remember
but I wonder
how to pass on.

Mark Boyer knows how to "pass on." He has passed on an engaging book of biblical passages, reflections and prayers. *A Month-by-Month Guide to Entertaining Angels* accompanies us through the year and spells out the different ways that God walks with people through the medium of angelic messengers. Angels, we discover again and again, are the way the transcendent God guides wayward earthlings toward salvation. Perhaps this is why Meister Eckhart said, "That's all an angel is, an idea of God."

Of course, God's ideas are not the idle thoughts we dally with. God's ideas manifest themselves in the phenomenal world and shine among us. Welcome to the shining world of angels.

Introduction

The title of this book comes from a Bible story about three mysterious visitors who dropped in, unannounced, on Abraham and Sarah one hot afternoon as they were taking a siesta. This is how the story is told in the Book of Genesis:

> The LORD appeared to Abraham by the oaks of Mamre, as he sat at the entrance of his tent in the heat of the day. He looked up and saw three men standing near him. When he saw them, he ran from the tent entrance to meet them, and bowed down to the ground. He said, "My lord, if I find favor with you, do not pass by your servant. Let a little water be brought, and wash your feet, and rest yourselves under the tree. Let me bring a little bread, that you may refresh yourselves, and after that you may pass on—since you have come to your servant."

> So they said, "Do as you have said." And Abraham hastened into the tent to Sarah, and said, "Make ready three measures of choice flour, knead it, and make cakes." Abraham ran to the herd, and took a calf, tender and good, and gave it to the servant, who hastened to prepare it. Then he took curds and milk and the calf that he had prepared, and set it before them; and he stood by them under the tree while they ate.

> They said to him, "Where is your wife Sarah?" And he said, "There, in the tent." Then one said, "I will surely return to you in due season, and your wife Sarah shall have a son." And Sarah was listening at the tent entrance behind him.

> Now Abraham and Sarah were old, advanced in age; it had ceased to be with Sarah after the manner of women. So Sarah laughed to herself, saying, "After I have grown old, and my husband is old, shall I have pleasure?"

> The LORD said to Abraham, "Why did Sarah laugh, and say, 'Shall I indeed bear a child, now that I am old?' Is anything too wonderful for the LORD? At the set time I will return to you, in due season, and Sarah shall have a son." But Sarah denied, saying, "I did not laugh"; for she was afraid. He said, "Oh yes, you did laugh."

Genesis 18:1-15

Who were these three strangers who knew so much about Abraham and Sarah's private life—and about the future? The story-teller calls one of them "the LORD," and the word he uses shows he means not just a human lord or ruler, but God. The other two visitors were angels: the author makes this clear as he continues to narrate their journey. "The two angels came to Sodom in the evening," he writes, "and Lot was sitting in the gateway of Sodom" (Genesis 19:1).

Many generations later, this story of Abraham, Sarah, and the three surprise callers reappears in the New Testament. Reflecting on Abraham and Sarah's lavish hospitality, the author of the Letter to the Hebrews tells his readers, "Do not neglect to show hospitality to strangers, for by doing that some have entertained angels without knowing it" (Hebrews 13:2).

Stop for a moment and look at the amazing implications of that statement. Abraham and Sarah, by offering hospitality to three strangers, entertained God and two angels and received the promise of a son—without fully recognizing who their visitors were!

This book is designed to help all of us entertain angels. By looking at how others have welcomed messengers from God, and by reflecting on passages from the Bible that tell about angels, we can grow in knowledge of how we too may welcome God's messengers—indeed, God himself—today. (Like angels, God is pure spirit and therefore neither male nor female. Yet God is also personal, in the same sense that humans and angels are separate, individual beings. To emphasize the personal nature of God, I will follow the bibilical convention of using masculine pronouns when referring to God.)

But before we start roasting a calf for our anticipated guests we will first take a quick look at angelology, the study of angels. Only a few highlights of that discipline are presented; to go into it in depth would require another whole book. It is important, however, to know some-thing about the idea of angels before we begin looking at individual angels themselves.

We will then be ready to meet and meditate on thirty-six angels whose stories are told in the Bible—three angels a month for us to entertain, just as Abraham and Sarah did, in the comfort of our homes. We will start by reading the angel stories as they are told in Scripture. Then we will follow each angel story with a reflection, some questions for meditation or for journaling, and a prayer.

The *Scripture passage* has been chosen to coincide as closely as possible with the liturgical year. Thus, for example, the stories we read in April reflect the themes of the Easter Season. In September, when the Church celebrates the Feast of the Archangels, we will entertain Michael, Gabriel, and Raphael. The angels associated with Christmas are our guests for December.

The *reflection* offers some background to the Scripture passage and some suggestions for understanding it. The reflection also expands ideas and images found in the verses from Scripture.

The questions for personal *meditation* or for journaling guide us in further developing and applying the ideas or images from the Scripture passages. The final question for each meditation—Who was the "angel" you entertained?—asks us to become aware of the many ways God has been present in our lives. When we see how God has acted in the past, we learn to recognize God's visits in the present and expect to see God in the future.

A *prayer* then summarizes the theme of the angel story from Scripture. The prayer is usually a selection from a Psalm or from another part of the Bible. It concludes our experience of entertaining angels by bringing together the scriptural theme, the reflection, and the insights gained from personal meditation or journaling.

I hope this book will reawaken and sensitize us to God's many visitations throughout every day. By showing hospitality, Abraham and Sarah entertained God and two angels without knowing it. Through our hospitality, we too, can welcome the divine presence—God in disguise—into our homes and lives.

A Brief Survey of Angelology

Artistic depictions of angels, though always available in museums and libraries, seem to increase and multiply from mid-November until early January. White-robed, round-faced, double-winged, part-human, part-bird creatures perch on the tops of Christmas trees and dangle from their branches. Suspended by picture-hanging wire, they hover over creches, bearing banners that say *Gloria in excelsis Deo*—"Glory to God in the highest." Sometimes they kneel and adore the child sleeping on straw in the manger.

Angels stream across Christmas cards blowing trumpets or strumming harps or simply looking concerned. And in grocery stores and elevators, restaurants and malls, we hear angels singing glory to the newborn King, greeting him with anthems sweet, sweetly singing o'er the plains, bending near the earth to touch their harps of gold, winging their flight o'er all the earth to proclaim Messiah's birth—and so on.

Although less aggressively than at Christmastime, angels make another appearance during the Easter season. On cards and book jackets they sit at the edge of an above-ground, lidless tomb, awaiting the arrival of a few fearful women who, in the background, are sneaking into the cemetery as the sun peeks over the horizon. The angels' tunics are bleached white, and their faces glow. They are about to announce that the Crucified One has been raised from the dead.

Christmas and Easter angels have inspired a whole industry of blonde-haired, rosy-cheeked, white-clothed figurines; cheerful little lapel pins; wall plaques and pictures; and lavishly illustrated books of inspiration and comfort. Nowadays, angels are everywhere. But if we investigate the etymology of the word *angel*, we discover an interesting fact: *Angel* was not originally a noun but a verb.

Angel Verbs

The English noun *angel* is a translation of the Greek *angelos*, which means "messenger," "one who is sent," or "one who brings a message." *Angelos* in the New Testament is the translation of the Hebrew *mal'ak*, used in the Old Testament to mean "messenger" or "angel." *Mal'ak*, in turn, is derived from *le'ak*, a verb meaning "to send" in Ugaritic, Arabic, and Ethiopic. The ancient writers of Scripture probably would not have recognized the anthropomorphic creatures we call angels.

Angels looking like winged men emanate from a time when people believed in a three-storied universe—heaven above, earth in the middle, the underworld below. Before airplanes were invented, the only creatures who could soar above the earth were birds. Since angels were believed to be messengers from the world above, where God lives, to the world in the middle, where people live, they were usually pictured with wings, the only known means of travel from one story of the universe to another.

We humans like to define reality in a way that lets us control it. We crave pictures, figurines, icons. And so, although the etymological root of *angel* is a verb describing God's activity, we have harnessed God's message-bearers and made them into winged humans that we can paint or sculpt. But a picture, a figurine, or an icon cannot adequately convey action, and the concept *angel* cannot be adequately drawn on paper, painted on a chapel ceiling, or molded in plaster of paris.

In this book, we are not going to look at angels as we humans have trapped or created them, more or less in our own image. Instead, we are going to look at angels in motion, angels without boundaries, angels as the eternal and myriad possibilities of God revealing himself to people. The God who reveals himself is not static; he is always Being-in-revelation, as we can see from the name God reveals to Moses.

In the Exodus, the second book of the Bible, Moses first encounters God on "Horeb, the mountain of God" (Exodus 3:1). The text continues, "There the angel of the LORD appeared to him in a flame of fire out of a bush" (Exodus 3:2). However, after Moses decided to walk over toward the flaming bush, "God called to him out of the bush, 'Moses, Moses!'" (Exodus 3:4). Clearly "the angel of the LORD" and "God" are synonymous.

Later in the narrative, Moses asks God for his name. God replies, "I AM WHO I AM" (Exodus 3:14), or *Yahweh*. The name is derived from an archaic form of the verb "to be." God is Being itself, and God cannot be controlled. Thus the angel of the Lord—in this case, God himself—reveals God's person and God's character to Moses.

We humans have tried to define and depict angels, but angels cannot be limited by our representations. *Angel*—originally "sending," then "messenger"—is shorthand for the unlimited ways God reveals himself to human beings. And just as God is beyond our understanding, so also are angels incomprehensible. Neither our intellect nor our imagination can begin to grasp the infinitude of God. However, we can speak about God's activity of constant revelation of himself by using the theological term *angel*.

6

From another perspective, we can look at *angel* as a metaphor, a word revealing God. Angels, then, are mirrors reflecting God's essence. They are thoughts to which God gives expression. They are hands God uses to reach out to people. Metaphorically, angels are God's myriad efforts to reach out to us.

Choirs of Angels

Humans love to order things. We have CEOs and vice presidents, genus and species, the periodic table of the elements. Theologians have ranked angels into choirs, or orders, organized into hierarchies. After gleaning and cataloguing the angelic names from the Bible, Pope St. Gregory I, also known as Gregory the Great (540-604 CE), identified nine choirs: Angels, Archangels, Principalities (Rulers), Virtues, Powers, Dominations, Thrones, Cherubim, and Seraphim.

About a century later, St. John Damascene (ca 675-749 CE) organized the nine choirs of angels into three triplex groups, or hierarchies. The highest group, consisting of those angels who are always in God's presence, includes Seraphim, Cherubim, and Thrones. The middle group is made up of Dominations, Powers, and Virtues. And the last group consists of Principalities, Archangels, and Angels.

The Office and Nature of Angels

It is not hard to see why angels, whose name is derived from a verb meaning "send," are seen as beings whose office, or function, is to transmit God's messages to people. As messengers, angels are servants of God's will.

God's messengers have a nature like God's: incorporeal and immaterial. That is, angels do not have physical bodies like ours, and they are not composed of matter. As created manifestations of God, they are pure spirits; yet they are also personal beings possessing intelligence, free will, and immortality. Because they are purely spiritual creatures having no physical matter, they do not suffer bodily corruption.

In our feeble attempt to understand the angelic manifestations of God, our whole concept of substance gets shattered. We must create metaphors or similes saying what angels must be like, knowing that our comparisons only faintly reflect who they really are.

Although both angels and humans are creatures, because humans exist in time and space we tend to "locate" angels somewhere between God and us. In the intermediary world where angels "live," they seem

7

little different from God. "The angel of the Lord," as we have seen in the accounts of Abraham and Sarah and Moses, is synonymous with God's action of self-revelation in some visible form.

Honoring Angels

We honor angels because in so doing, we honor God—angels are God's manifestations. The Second Vatican Council proposed that the Church continue to venerate angels. In Chapter VII of *The Dogmatic Constitution of the Church*, "The Pilgrim Church," the bishops declare that the Church has always venerated the holy angels and asked for their help. Echoing this document, the new catechism of the Catholic Church similarly emphasizes that all human life is surrounded by the watchful care and intercession of angels.

The Roman Catholic Church devotes two days of the liturgical year to honoring angels. On September 29 the Feast of the Archangels—Michael, Gabriel, and Raphael—is celebrated, while on October 2 the Church honors guardian angels. The preface of the Eucharistic Prayer for both of those days emphasizes that angels are manifestations of God. Addressing the all-powerful and ever-living God, the minister prays: "In praising your faithful angels and archangels, we also praise your glory, for in honoring them, we honor you, their creator. Their splendor shows us your greatness, which surpasses in goodness the whole of creation" (*The Sacramentary*, Preface 60, page 493).

The Church also honors the angels by singing their "Holy, Holy, Holy" after the preface of every Mass. In Eucharistic Prayer I, the priest asks that God's angel carry the sacrifice of the body and blood of Christ from our earthly altar to the heavenly altar. As part of the closing of the Mass of Christian Burial, we ask that angels lead the deceased into paradise.

In a Nutshell

In this brief survey of angelology, we have seen that the word *angel* is derived from an ancient verb meaning "to send." In theological discourse, angel narratives refer to God's ongoing self-revelation. God has from the beginning of time been in the process of revealing himself to people, so it is not surprising that angels are numerous. Their function is to be messengers of God's self-revelation.

It is time now to begin entertaining angels, looking for what they have to reveal to us about God.

THREE ANGELS

FOR

JANUARY

God Saves

God Instructs

God Reveals the Future

God Saves

The two angels [whom, along with the Lord, Abraham had accompanied from his tent toward Sodom and Gomorrah] came to Sodom in the evening, and Lot was sitting in the gate of Sodom. When Lot saw them, he rose to meet them and bowed down with his face to the ground. He said, "Please, my lords, turn aside to your servant's house and spend the night, and wash your feet; then you can rise early and go on your way." They said, "No; we will spend the night in the square." But he urged them strongly; so they turned aside to him and entered his house; and he made them a feast, and baked unleavened bread, and they ate.

Then the men said to Lot, "Have you anyone else here? Sons-in-law, sons, daughters, or anyone you have in the city— bring them out of the place. For we are about to destroy this place, because the outcry against its people has become great before the LORD, and the LORD has sent us to destroy it."

When morning dawned, the angels urged Lot, saying, "Get up, take your wife and your two daughters who are here, or else you will be consumed in the punishment of the city." But he lingered; so the men seized him and his wife and his two daughters by the hand, the LORD being merciful to him, and they brought him out and left him outside the city.

The sun had risen on the earth . . . . Then the LORD rained on Sodom and Gomorrah sulphur and fire from the LORD out of heaven . . . .

Abraham went early in the morning to the place where he had stood before the LORD; and he looked down toward Sodom and Gomorrah and toward all the land of the Plain and saw the smoke of the land going up like the smoke of a furnace.

So it was that, when God destroyed the cities of the Plain, God remembered Abraham, and sent Lot out of the midst of the overthrow, when he overthrew the cities in which Lot had settled.

Genesis 19:1-3, 12-13, 15-16, 23-24, 27-29

REflecTioN

This story picks up where the story of Abraham and Sarah's three heavenly visitors leaves off. The story-teller makes a deliberate parallel between Abraham's reception of three strangers and Lot's reception of two. Abraham welcomes God himself, while Lot receives God's two messengers. Abraham is promised that his line will continue through the birth of a son; Lot is told to take his family and flee Sodom so that his line does not die out when the city is destroyed.

The focus of this narrative, however, is on Lot's salvation. God, through the two angel-messengers, saves Lot from death. He does this because Lot is related to Abraham.

The God of Abraham and Lot is a God who wants to befriend people, who desires to save people if they will cooperate with him. How do we cooperate with God? Cooperation begins with hospitality, welcoming God in the person of messengers into our home. Then we must listen to their message. Finally we need to act on what we have heard, even though we may not understand it fully. These three steps—welcoming, listening, acting—form the biblical basis for the proper response to God's angel-messengers. The result is always salvation.

Abraham welcomed three visitors to his tent. He listened to their message that he and Sarah would conceive a son. He acted on what he was told. Because of Abraham and Sarah's trust, nine months later Isaac was born. God formed his chosen people, from whom came the Savior of the world.

Lot welcomed two visitors to his home. He listened to their message that he and his family should flee Sodom. He left the city, as he had been instructed. Because of Lot's trust, he and his daughters escaped the destructive fire of Sodom and Gomorrah. God saved his people.

Remember Lot's wife? She failed to act on what she heard. The Lord's messengers had told Lot, his wife, and his daughters, "Do not look back or stop anywhere in the plain" (Genesis 19:17). "But Lot's wife, behind him, looked back, and she became a pillar of salt" (Genesis 19:26).

God desires to save us, just as he saved Abraham and Lot. God is always in the process of sending angel-messengers to guide us to salvation. When we entertain them, we receive a message. When we listen to and act on their words, we discover that it was the divine presence—God himself—who was seeking our friendship in order to save us.

MEDITATION

➤ When have you most recently welcomed a messenger from God, listened to the message, and acted on what you heard?

➤ From what did God save you?

➤ Who was the "angel" you entertained?

PRAYER

I will bless the LORD at all times;

his praise shall continually be in my mouth.

My soul makes its boast in the LORD;

let the humble hear me and be glad.

O magnify the LORD with me,

let us exalt his name together.

I sought the LORD, and he answered me

and delivered me from all my fears.

Look to him, and be radiant;

so your faces shall never be ashamed.

This poor soul cried, and was heard by the LORD,

and was saved from every trouble.

The angel of the LORD encamps

around those who fear him, and delivers them.

O taste and see that the LORD is good;

happy are those who take refuge in him.

Psalm 34:1-8

God Instructs

SCRIPTURE

Sarai dealt harshly with [Hagar], and she ran away from her.

The angel of the LORD found her by a spring of water in the wilderness . . . . And he said, "Hagar, slave-girl of Sarai, where have you come from and where are you going?" She said, "I am running away from my mistress Sarai." The angel of the LORD said to her, "Return to your mistress, and submit to her." The angel of the LORD also said to her, "I will so greatly multiply your offspring that they cannot be counted for multitude." And the angel of the LORD said to her,

"Now you have conceived and shall bear a son;

you shall name him Ishmael,

for the LORD has given heed to your affliction."

So she named the LORD who spoke to her, "You are El-roi"; for she said, "Have I really seen God and remained alive after seeing him?"

Hagar bore Abram a son; and Abram named his son, whom Hagar bore, Ishmael.

The LORD dealt with Sarah as he had said, and the LORD did for Sarah as he had promised. Sarah conceived and bore Abraham a son in his old age, at the time of which God had spoken to him. Abraham gave the name Isaac to his son whom Sarah bore him.

Sarah saw the son of Hagar the Egyptian, whom she had borne to Abraham, playing with her son Isaac. So she said to Abraham, "Cast out this slave woman with her son; for the son of this slave woman shall not inherit along with my son Isaac." The matter was very distressing to Abraham on account of his son. But God said to Abraham, "Do not be distressed because of the boy and because of your slave woman; whatever Sarah says to you, do as she tells you, for it is through Isaac that offspring shall be named for you. As for the son of the slave woman, I will make a nation of him also, because he is your offspring."

So Abraham rose early in the morning, and took bread and a skin of water, and gave it to Hagar, putting it on her shoulder, along with the child, and sent her away. And she departed, and wandered about in the wilderness . . . .

When the water in the skin was gone, she cast the child under one of the bushes. Then she went and sat down opposite him a good way off, about the distance of a bowshot; for she said, "Do not let me look on the death of the child." And as she sat opposite him, she lifted up her voice and wept. And God heard the voice of the boy; and the angel of the LORD called to Hagar from heaven, and said to her, "What troubles you, Hagar? Do not be afraid; for God has heard the voice of the boy where he is. Come, lift up the boy and hold him fast with your hand, for I will make a great nation of him." Then God opened her eyes and she saw a well of water. She went, and filled the skin with water, and gave the boy a drink.

God was with the boy, and he grew up; he lived in the wilderness, and became an expert with the bow.

Genesis 16:6-11, 13, 15; 21:1-3, 9-20

REfLECTION

This is a story of tangled family relationships—the patriarch Abraham; his wife, Sarah, and their son, Isaac; Sarah's handmaid, Hagar, and her son by Abraham, Ishmael. In the midst of this confusing and often bitter situation, God is revealed as one who instructs and directs the lives of his people. His care is especially direct in the case of the outcasts Hagar and Ishmael, who have no other resources on which to rely.

The angel of the Lord—God in disguise—meets Hagar and Ishmael, gives them messages, and then departs. The angel of the Lord mediates the divine word. The angel is not a being like God or somewhat lower than God. The angel is the word of God, the act of God, touching the earth.

Notice how the story-teller speaks as if God, the Lord, and the angel of the Lord are all the same. He speaks of God appearing instead of an angel, and of an angel appearing in place of God, as a way of expressing God's touching the earth.

14

The Lord's angel tells the fugitive and pregnant Hagar to return to her mistress, Sarah, even though Sarah had harassed her and provoked her to flee. Dying of thirst in the wilderness, Hagar receives a promise from God: She will be the mother of a son who will, in turn, be the father of a great nation. Her son will be named Ishmael, "May God hear." Hagar's son will be the embodied sign of God's instruction and promise, of hope in the midst of suffering.

Hagar obeys the angel-messenger and returns to Sarah, but not until she names the Lord—that is, the Lord's messenger— *El-roi*, "God of seeing" or "God who sees." God, in the person of the angel, has seen Hagar's distress and is rescuing her through his instructive word.

After Ishmael is born to Hagar and Isaac to Sarah, Sarah becomes jealous of Ishmael and provokes Abraham to send him away with his mother into the wilderness. Soon Hagar and Ishmael run out of bread and water, and they prepare to die.

Once again, an angel comes to the rejected Hagar. "God heard the voice of the boy," says the story-teller. "God heard"—an echo of Ishmael's name!

And once again, an angel brings Hagar God's words. The angel tells Hagar not to fear: The boy will survive. God will make a great nation from him. Just as God has heard Hagar in her times of greatest need and instructed her action, so God will hear Hagar's son and instruct him.

God's word has touched the earth. It has instructed both Hagar and Ishmael through the mediation of an angel.

MEDITATION

> ➤ How has God's word instructed or guided you through the mediation of another?

> ➤ What did God tell you?

> ➤ How did you respond?

> ➤ Who was the "angel" you entertained?

PRAYER

The LORD has established his throne in the heavens,

and his kingdom rules over all.

Bless the LORD, O you his angels,

you mighty ones who do his bidding,

obedient to his spoken word.

Bless the LORD, all his hosts,

his ministers that do his will.

Bless the LORD, all his works,

in all places of his dominion.

Bless the LORD, O my soul.

Psalm 103:19-22

God Reveals the Future

Jacob. . . came to a certain place and stayed there for the night, because the sun had set. Taking one of the stones of the place, he put it under his head and lay down in that place. And he dreamed that there was a ladder set up on the earth, the top of it reaching to heaven; and the angels of God were ascending and descending on it. And the LORD stood beside him and said, "I am the LORD, the God of Abraham your father and the God of Isaac; the land on which you lie I will give to you and to your offspring; and your offspring shall be like the dust of the earth, and you shall spread abroad to the west and to the east and to the north and to the south; and all the families of the earth shall be blessed in you and in your offspring. Know that I am with you and will keep you wherever you go, and will bring you back to this land; for I will not leave you until I have done what I have promised you."

Then Jacob awoke from his sleep and said, "Surely the LORD is in this place—and I did not know it!" And he was afraid, and said, "How awesome is this place! This is none other than the house of God, and this is the gate of heaven!" So Jacob rose early in the morning, and he took the stone that he had put under his head and set it up for a pillar and poured oil on top of it. He called that place Bethel . . . .

Then Jacob made a vow, saying, "If God will be with me, and will keep me in this way that I go, and will give me bread to eat and clothing to wear, so that I come again to my father's house in peace, then the LORD shall be my God, and this stone, which I have set up for a pillar, shall be God's house."

Genesis 28:10-22

REFLECTION

Jacob dreams of a ladder, or stairway, that is planted on the earth and reaches to heaven. It is a link between heaven and earth. On the ladder, angels (messengers) go up and down. The ladder and the angels allow God to make contact with human beings. Through this dream, God contacts Jacob.

Look at how the story-teller sets the scene: first Jacob sees the ladder with the angels; then suddenly the Lord himself stands beside him. First a vision; then a *theophany*, an appearance of God. The Lord speaks to Jacob. He renews the original promises made to Abraham. Jacob will receive land and descendants, and through the descendants all nations of the earth will be blessed. God reassures Jacob and reveals his future to him.

Once he has entertained angels, Jacob awakens. First, he recognizes the divine presence. Second, he responds with awesome fear. Third, he ritually dedicates the place to God by anointing the stone that he used for a pillow the night before. Jacob then names the spot *Bethel*, "house of God." He now recognizes that the place where he encountered God and God revealed his future is "the gate of heaven." The theophany—the Lord's appearance on earth—assures Jacob of the Lord's continuous presence in heaven.

The Book of Genesis tells another story in which God contacts Jacob through an angel. Years after the dream of the angel-ladder, after Jacob has married Leah and Rachel and worked half a lifetime for his father-in-law, he begins the journey back to his homeland, where his estranged brother Esau lives. Before meeting with his brother, Jacob meets God again.

During the night, "a man wrestled with him until daybreak. When the man saw that he did not prevail against Jacob, he struck him on the hip socket; and Jacob's hip was put out of joint as he wrestled with him. Then he said, 'Let me go, for the day is break-ing.' But Jacob said, 'I will not let you unless you bless me.' So he said to him, 'What is your name?' And he said, 'Jacob.' Then the man said, 'You shall no longer be called Jacob, but Israel, for you have striven with God and with humans, and have prevailed.' Then Jacob asked him, 'Please tell me your name.' But he said, 'Why is it that you ask my name?' And there he blessed him. So Jacob called the place Peniel, saying, 'For I have seen God face to face, and yet my life is preserved'" (Genesis 32:24-31).

The man-become-angel-become-God gives Jacob a new name—*Israel*—"may God rule" or "you have struggled." In turn, Jacob names the place where the wrestling match was held *Peniel*, "face of God." Jacob claims a lesser victory than God's; Jacob is happy to have had his life spared. However, his life is spared for his future, which God once again reveals to him.

Through the angels, God's messengers, Jacob-renamed-Israel has been contacted by God, recognized God's presence, responded to God with awe, dedicated places to God, wrestled with God, seen God's face, and received a revelation of his future from God. Truly, Jacob is blessed by God.

MEDITATION

> ➤ Where have you most recently recognized God's presence?

> ➤ How did you respond to it?

> ➤ Was there any wrestling involved?

> ➤ How did you dedicate the place that was your ladder or gate of heaven?

> ➤ What revelation about your future did you receive?

> ➤ Who was the "angel" you entertained?

PRAYER

I give you thanks, O LORD, with my whole heart;

before the gods I sing your praise;

I bow down toward your holy temple

and give thanks to your name

for your steadfast love and your faithfulness;

for you have exalted your name and your word

above everything.

On the day I called, you answered me,

you increased my strength of soul.

Psalm 138:1-3

THREE ANGELS

FOR

FEBRUARY

God Unveils

God Strengthens

God Gives Life

God Unveils

That night God came to Balaam and said to him, "If the men have come to summon you, get up and go with them; but do only what I tell you to do." So Balaam got up in the morning, saddled his donkey, and went with the officials of Moab.

God's anger was kindled because he was going, and the angel of the LORD took his stand in the road as his adversary. Now he was riding on his donkey, and his two servants were with him. The donkey saw the angel of the LORD standing in the road, with a drawn sword in his hand; so the donkey turned off the road, and went into the field; and Balaam struck the donkey, to turn it back onto the road. Then the angel of the LORD stood in a narrow path between the vineyards, with a wall on either side. When the donkey saw the angel of the LORD , it scraped against the wall, and scraped Balaam's foot against the wall; so he struck it again. Then the angel of the LORD went ahead, and stood in a narrow place, where there was no way to turn either to the right or to the left. When the donkey saw the angel of the LORD , it lay down under Balaam; and Balaam's anger was kindled, and he struck the donkey with his staff. Then the LORD opened the mouth of the donkey, and it said to Balaam, "What have I done to you, that you have struck me these three times?" Balaam said to the donkey, "Because you have made a fool of me! I wish I had a sword in my hand! I would kill you right now." But the donkey said to Balaam, "Am I not your donkey, which you have ridden all your life to this day? Have I been in the habit of treating you this way?" And he said, "No."

Then the LORD opened the eyes of Balaam, and he saw the angel of the LORD standing in the road with his drawn sword in his hand; and he bowed down, falling on his face. The angel of the LORD said to him, "Why have you struck your donkey these three times? I have come out as an adversary, because your way is perverse before me. The donkey saw me, and turned away from me these three times. If it had not turned away from me, surely just now I would have killed you and let it live." Then

Balaam said to the angel of the LORD , "I have sinned, for I did not know that you were standing in the road to oppose me. Now therefore, if it is displeasing to you, I will return home." The angel of the LORD said to Balaam, "Go with the men; but speak only what I tell you to speak." So Balaam went on with the officials of Balak.

Numbers 22:20-35

REfLECTION

The verb *convert* means "to turn around." A converted person takes a new course of action, or understands something from a new perspective, or accepts a previously unthinkable idea, or loves what was once hated or ignored. In some cases conversion takes place immediately, while in other cases it takes a few years or even a lifetime.

It may take awhile to turn around, because we get comfortable with our own ideas and behaviors and prefer them to new thoughts and actions. When others challenge our comfortable way of life, we bristle. How similar we are to Balaam, the prophet summoned by King Balak to curse the Israelites! Did Balaam really think that God was going to permit him to curse God's chosen people? Through an angel's intercession, God converts Balaam, lifts the veil from his eyes. Balaam turns around and blesses Israel.

The angel of the Lord mediates God's revelation to Balaam. Angels protect the divine transcendence by making direct contact unnecessary between God and human beings. But this angel speaks and is spoken of as if it is identical with God. Even though Balaam is less perceptive than his donkey, God is able to turn him around so that he does God's will. God unveils Balaam's blindness.

The donkey is more sensitive to the presence of God's messenger than is Balaam. The beast of burden senses the approach of the angel and gets out of the way. But Balaam is totally clueless. Even though he is a prophet of God, his eyes have to be opened so that he can detect the angel's presence. Had the donkey not turned aside, the angel's sword would have struck Balaam. He had the animal to thank that he survived the confrontation.

Once Balaam is turned around, he expresses a desire to go back home. But God is not interested in that. To turn around, to have the veil lifted from one's eyes, means that one cannot go backward. God sends Balaam to the Moabite king, Balak, in whose presence Balaam will do God's bidding by three times blessing Israel's camps and by declaring:

> I see him, but not now;
>
> > I behold him, but not near—
>
> a star shall come out of Jacob,
>
> > and a scepter shall rise out of Israel;
>
> it shall crush the borderlands of Moab,
>
> > . . . while Israel does valiantly.
>
> One out of Jacob shall rule.

Numbers 24:17-19

Balaam's words about "a star" advancing "out of Jacob" and "a scepter" rising "out of Israel" refer to monarchy. Balaam's oracle has been applied to the reign of David as well as to that of Christ. The man who once agreed to curse Israel made a 180-degree turn and gave Israel one of its most celebrated blessings. When Balaam entertained an angel, God converted him and lifted the veil from his eyes.

MEDITATION

➤ When have you recently experienced being converted or "turned around"?

➤ What veil was lifted from your eyes regarding an idea, a perspective, a position, etc.?

➤ Who was the "angel" you entertained?

PRAYER

God is not a human being, that he should lie,

> or a mortal, that he should change his mind.

Has he promised, and will he not do it?

Has he spoken, and will he not fulfill it?

See, I received a command to bless;

> he has blessed, and I cannot revoke it.

He has not beheld misfortune in Jacob;

> nor has he seen trouble in Israel.

The LORD their God is with them,

> acclaimed as a king among them.

God, who brings them out of Egypt,

> is like the horns of a wild ox for them.

Surely there is no enchantment against Jacob,

> no divination against Israel;

> now it shall be said of Jacob and Israel,

'See what God has done!'

Look, a people rising up like a lioness,

> and rousing itself like a lion!

It does not lie down until it has eaten the prey

> and drunk the blood of the slain.

Numbers 23:19-24

God Strengthens

SCRIPTURE

Now the angel of the LORD came and sat under the oak . . . as . . . Gideon was beating out wheat in the wine press to hide it from the Midianites. The angel of the LORD appeared to him and said to him, "The LORD is with you, you mighty warrior." Gideon answered him, "But sir, if the LORD is with us, why then has all this happened to us? And where are his wonderful deeds that our ancestors recounted to us . . . ? But now the LORD has cast us off, and given us into the hand of Midian."

Then the LORD turned to him and said, "Go in this might of yours and deliver Israel from the hand of Midian; I hereby commission you . . . . I will be with you, and you shall strike down the Midianites, every one of them." Then he said to him, "If now I have found favor with you, show me a sign that it is you who speak with me. Do not depart from me here until I come to you, and bring out my present, and set it before you." And he said, "I will stay until you return."

So Gideon went into his house and prepared a kid, and unleavened cakes from an ephah of flour; the meat he put in a basket, and the broth he put in a pot, and brought them to him under the oak and presented them. The angel of God said to him, "Take the meat and the unleavened cakes, and put them on this rock, and pour out the broth." And he did so. Then the angel of the LORD reached out the tip of the staff that was in his hand, and touched the meat and the unleavened cakes; and fire sprang up from the rock and consumed the meat and the unleavened cakes; and the angel of the LORD vanished from his sight. Then Gideon perceived that it was the angel of the LORD; and Gideon said, "Help me, Lord GOD! For I have seen the angel of the LORD face to face!" But the LORD said him, "Peace be to you; do not fear, you shall not die."

Judges 6:11-14, 16-23

REfLECTION

The angel of the Lord appears to Gideon as a solitary divine messenger. Gideon, not sure whether he can trust this purported agent from God, asks for a sign, some proof of authenticity. He receives his sign when his offering is consumed by fire.

Perhaps the fire reminded Gideon of stories about Israel's mighty leader, Moses, who first met God in a burning bush. Like Moses, Gideon has a profound religious experience. It is from this experience of God's presence that Gideon draws strength to do God's will by saving Israel from its enemies, the Midianites.

How often we, like Gideon, must face what looks like an impossible situation. We try pretending that the problem is not there in the hope that it will go away or solve itself. When this strategy wears thin, we may get angry at the thought that our situation is still grim. Our anger may lead us to punish ourselves and others. But after days, weeks, months, or even years of frustration, we eventually find that we have to deal with the situation. And then we may find that the strength we need has been there all along; all we have to do is ask God to send an angel to deliver it to us, just as God sent an angel to Gideon.

Our world today is filled with stressful situations that cry out for divine intervention. Some of these stresses are major crises: death, divorce, desertion, unemployment, abuse, addictions. But many come from what passes for normal daily life.

In the home, it seems there is never enough time for loving relationships to grow and be nurtured. Perhaps there is only one adult in the family, or both parents must work full time, or there are too many young or old or ill people demanding constant attention. Household jobs pile up—mowing the lawn, washing clothes, going to the grocery store, supervising children, paying bills.

In the workplace, increasing demands make it hard to do any job well. Employers ask more and more from employees. Many company policies do not adequately meet workers' needs. A changing economy threatens everyone's job security.

It is easy to see why we need to entertain an angel of strength.

It is important to note that, in Gideon's story, God makes the first move. God sends the angel of the Lord to Gideon while Gideon is busily trying to save some of the wheat harvest from his people's enemies. The angel tells Gideon that God is with him. When Gideon asks for a sign, God cooperates and provides one—the consuming fire.

What Gideon learns is that God is present. In fact God has always been present. All Gideon has to do is to entertain the strengthening divine presence.

The same is true for us. God is present with us. All we need to do is become aware of God's strengthening intervention in our stress-filled lives. When faced with problems, we are often tempted to ignore or run away from whatever is troubling us. The lesson God teaches through Gideon is that we need to reverse this tendency. Rather than giving in to our weakness and running away, we should face our fears and then open ourselves more than ever to the strength God wants to lavish upon us. Put simply, we need to entertain the angel of the Lord, to welcome God into our lives, and to discover that there is no cause for fear. We are not alone. In fact, God strengthens us to pursue whatever God wants of us.

At his time of greatest weakness and fear, Jesus opened himself to God. On the Mount of Olives, according to Luke's Gospel, Jesus prayed, "Father, if you are willing, remove this cup from me; yet not my will but yours be done" (Luke 22:42). Then, the author continues, "an angel from heaven appeared to him and gave him strength" (Luke 22:43).

If God's own Son needed to appeal to his Father for strength, how much more do we need to invite God into our lives. And God *will* strengthen us, just as he strengthened Gideon and Jesus, if we but entertain his angel.

MEDITATION

> ➤ In what stressful situation have you recently found yourself?
> ➤ Did you retreat or open yourself up to God's strengthening presence?
> ➤ If you retreated, what did you learn about yourself?
> ➤ If you permitted God to strengthen you, who was the "angel" you entertained?

PRAYER

Be merciful to me, O God, be merciful to me,

for in you my soul takes refuge;

in the shadow of your wings I will take refuge,

until the destroying storms pass by.

I cry to God Most High,

to God who fulfills his purpose for me.

He will send from heaven and save me,

he will put to shame those who trample on me.

God will send forth his steadfast love

and his faithfulness.

Be exalted, O God, above the heavens.

Let your glory be over all the earth.

Psalm 57:1-3a, 5

God Gives Life

There was a certain man from Zorah, of the tribe of the Danites, whose name was Manoah. His wife was barren, having borne no children. And the angel of the LORD appeared to the woman and said to her, "Although you are barren, having borne no children, you shall conceive and bear a son. Now be careful not to drink wine or strong drink, or to eat anything unclean, for you shall conceive and bear a son. No razor is to come on his head, for the boy shall be a nazirite to God from birth. It is he who shall begin to deliver Israel from the hand of the Philistines."

Then the woman came and told her husband, "A man of God came to me, and his appearance was like that of an angel of God, most awe-inspiring; I did not ask him where he came from, and he did not tell me his name; but he said to me, 'You shall conceive and bear a son. So then drink no wine or strong drink, and eat nothing unclean, for the boy shall be a nazirite to God from birth to the day of his death.'"

Then Manoah entreated the LORD, and said, "O, LORD, I pray, let the man of God whom you sent come to us again and teach us what we are to do concerning the boy who will be born."

God listened to Manoah, and the angel of God came again to the woman as she sat in the field; but her husband Manoah was not with her. So the woman ran quickly and told her husband, "The man who came to me the other day has appeared to me." Manoah got up and followed his wife, and came to the man and he said to him, "Are you the man who spoke to this woman?" And he said, "I am."

Then Manoah said, "Now, when your words come true, what is to be the boy's rule of life; what is he to do?" The angel of the LORD said to Manoah, "Let the woman give heed to all that I said to her. She may not eat of anything that comes from the vine. She is not to drink wine or strong drink, or eat any unclean thing. She is to observe everything that I commanded her."

Manoah said to the angel of the LORD, "Allow us to detain you, and prepare a kid for you." The angel of the LORD said to Manoah, "If you detain me, I will not eat of your food; but if want to prepare a burnt offering, then offer it to the LORD." (For Manoah did not know that he was the angel of the LORD.) Then Manoah said to the angel of the LORD, "What is your name, so that we may honor you when your words come true?" But the angel of the LORD said to him, "Why do you ask my name? It is too wonderful."

So Manoah took the kid with the grain offering, and offered it on the rock to the LORD, to him who works wonders. When the flame went up toward heaven from the altar, the angel of the LORD ascended in the flame of the altar while Manoah and his wife looked on; and they fell on their faces to the ground. The angel of the LORD did not appear again to Manoah and his wife. Then Manoah realized that it was the angel of the LORD. And Manoah said to his wife, "We shall surely die, for we have seen God." But his wife said to him, "If the LORD had meant to kill us, he would not have accepted a burnt offering and a grain offering at our hands, or shown us all these things, or now announced to us such things as these."

The woman bore a son, and named him Samson. The boy grew, and the LORD blessed him.

Judges 13:2-24

REflECTION

God sent the angel of life to a barren woman, a woman who thought she was unable to give birth to a child!

This is a prominent theme in the Bible. We recall the story of Sarah who, when she is far past the age of childbearing, gives birth to Isaac. In the New Testament the aging Elizabeth, wife of Zechariah, gives birth to John the Baptizer. And young Mary, a virgin, gives birth to Jesus. In all three cases the women entertain an angel who brings God's promise of life.

This is also true of Manoah's wife, whose name is not recorded. She is barren, but the angel of the Lord tells her that she will conceive and bear a son. This son is to be consecrated from the womb as a Nazirite. He will not drink alcoholic beverages or consume any product of the vine. He will not be shaved. He will not touch dead bodies. In other words, this promised child—Samson—has been particularly chosen by God.

The messenger refuses to reveal his name, although Manoah's wife notes that his appearance is "awe inspiring," a description often used of God. The Hebrews believed that a person's power resides in his name. Whoever knows a person's name has power over him. The angel's anonymity, then, is a way of showing Manoah and his wife that they cannot control God's messenger.

The angel, as a manifestation of God, is incomprehensible, beyond human understanding. His mission is not to be understood by humans, but rather to reveal God to them. When Manoah asks the angel to stay for dinner, the angel refuses. He instructs Manoah to offer the food to the God of life, of whom the angel is a revelation.

Manoah goes ahead and prepares the kid and the grain, the traditional biblical tokens of hospitality presented to those who have traveled a long way. He lays the food out on a rock as an offering to God. Just as the smoke of the offering rises up to God, so too does the angel ascend in the flame.

Suddenly Manoah and his wife know that their suspicions were correct—the angel of the Lord has been God all along. Manoah is terrified that they, having seen God, will now die. His wife is more sensible. Why would the angel predict new life only to take it away?

God gave Manoah's wife the gift of bringing forth Samson's physical life. God gives us the gift of life also. The sight of an early morning sunrise over the mountaintops can revive us, give us new life, when we have felt harried and dragged down. Intimate sharing between friends can enhance the life of each one and inspire both to life-affirming action. When we have struggled long with an idea whose time has come, life can explode in creativity. And of course, the birth of a child to husband and wife is a culmination of shared life and a promise to nurture new life.

Thus does God give life through his angel-messengers, who teach us to worship the God of all life.

MEDITATION

> ➤ When did you most recently experience the gift of life from God?

> ➤ How were you empty or barren before receiving this life?

> ➤ How did you praise God for the gift of life?

> ➤ Who was the "angel" you entertained?

PRAYER

Bless the LORD, O my soul.

O LORD my God, you are very great.

You are clothed with honor and majesty,

    wrapped in light as with a garment.

You stretch out the heavens like a tent,

    you set the beams of your chambers on the waters,

    you make the clouds your chariot,

    you ride on the wings of the wind,

    you make the winds your messengers,

    fire and flame your ministers.

Psalm 104:1-4

THREE ANGELS

FOR

MARCH

God Sends on a Mission

God Feeds

God Repents

God Sends on a Mission

SCRIPTURE

Moses was keeping the flock of his father-in-law Jethro, the priest of Midian; he led his flock beyond the wilderness, and came to Horeb, the mountain of God. There the angel of the LORD appeared to him in a flame of fire out of a bush; he looked, and the bush was blazing, yet it was not consumed. Then Moses said, "I must turn aside and look at this great sight, and see why the bush is not burned up."

When the LORD saw that he had turned aside to see, God called to him out of the bush, "Moses! Moses!" And he said, "Here I am." Then he said, "Come no closer! Remove the sandals from your feet, for the place on which you are standing is holy ground." He said further, "I am the God of your father, the God of Abraham, the God of Isaac, and the God of Jacob." And Moses hid his face, for he was afraid to look at God.

Then the LORD said, "I have observed the misery of my people who are in Egypt; I have heard their cry on account of their taskmasters. Indeed, I know their sufferings, and I have come down to deliver them from the Egyptians, and to bring them up out of that land to a good and broad land, a land flowing with milk and honey . . . . So, come, I will send you to Pharaoh to bring my people, the Israelites, out of Egypt."

But Moses said to God, "Who am I that I should go to Pharaoh, and bring the Israelites out of Egypt?" He said, "I will be with you; and this shall be the sign for you that it is I who sent you: when you have brought the people out of Egypt, you shall worship God on this mountain."

Exodus 3:1-8, 10-12

REFLECTION

All of us have had the experience of being sent on a mission. As children we may have been sent by our parents from the den to the kitchen to get a glass of water. Once we got our driver's license, we may have been sent to the grocery store to pick up an item of

36

food for dinner. As adults, we send each other to get the mail, to have the car repaired, to take care of many daily tasks. Some of us are also aware that God has sent us on a mission. He has called us to do our work, to nurture relationships, to be a person of strong character, to live in his presence.

God sent Moses on a mission to the Pharaoh of Egypt, to lead the chosen people from slavery to freedom. God announced this mission through his messenger, the angel of the Lord, who confronted Moses on Horeb in the flame. This story of the burning bush is the first in a series of biblical stories in which God's messengers announce deliverance to God's people. In this story, God commissions Moses to begin the task of freeing his people.

The burning but unconsumed bush mediates the divine voice. Moses at first balks at his mission, but God encourages him with a promise: Once the Israelites have been freed, they will worship God on God's mountain. Years later, when the Israelites gathered for worship at Horeb (Sinai), they would remember the story of the burning bush and know that God had led them there.

God, called "the angel of the Lord," orders Moses to lead the Israelites out of Egypt into the land promised to Abraham and his descendants. Through his messenger to Moses, God claims the worship and obedience of his people. In Egypt, the people were bound to serve Pharaoh. In order to serve God, they would have to leave Egypt.

Moses' mission involved separation. First, Moses had to separate from his father-in-law and the flocks in Midian and go to Egypt. Second, Israel had to separate from Egypt and go to Sinai. Third, God, who had been quiet since the time of Israel's enslavement in Egypt, had to separate from his silence and honor the promises made to Abraham and his descendants forever. All these separations took place because Moses was willing to entertain the angel of the Lord and to accept the mission on which God sent him.

MEDITATION

> ➤ On what mission has God recently sent you?

> ➤ What sign before or after did you receive?

> ➤ What type of separation was involved?

> ➤ Who was the "angel" you entertained?

PRAYER

Praise the LORD!

Praise the name of the LORD;

    give praise, O servants of the LORD,

    you that stand in the house of the LORD,

    in the courts of the house of our God.

Praise the LORD, for the LORD is good;

    sing to his name, for he is gracious.

For the LORD has chosen Jacob for himself,

    Israel as his own possession.

For I know that the LORD is great;

    our Lord is above all gods.

Whatever the LORD pleases he does,

    in heaven and on earth,

    in the seas and all deeps.

He it was who struck down the firstborn of Egypt,

    both human beings and animals;

    he sent signs and wonders

    into your midst, O Egypt,

    against Pharaoh and all his servants.

. . . And gave their land as a heritage,

    a heritage to his people Israel.

Your name, O LORD, endures forever,

    your renown, O LORD, throughout all ages.

For the LORD will vindicate his people,

    and have compassion on his servants.

Psalm 135:1-6, 8-9, 12-14

God Feeds

[King] Ahab told [Queen] Jezebel all that Elijah had done, and how he had killed all the prophets [of Baal] with the sword. Then Jezebel sent a messenger to Elijah, saying, "So may the gods do to me, and more also, if I do not make your life like the life of one of them by this time tomorrow." Then he was afraid; he got up and fled for his life . . . .

But he . . . went a day's journey into the wilderness, and came and sat down under a solitary broom tree. He asked that he might die: "It is enough; now, O LORD, take away my life, for I am no better than my ancestors." Then he lay down under the broom tree and fell asleep.

Suddenly an angel touched him and said to him, "Get up and eat." He looked, and there at his head was a cake baked on hot stones, and a jar of water. He ate and drank, and lay down again. The angel of the LORD came a second time, touched him, and said, "Get up and eat, otherwise the journey will be too much for you!" He got up, and ate and drank; then he went in the strength of that food forty days and forty nights to Horeb the mount of God.

At that place he came to a cave, and spent the night there. Then the word of the LORD came to him, saying, "What are you doing here, Elijah?" He answered, "I have been very zealous for the LORD, the God of hosts; for the Israelites have forsaken your covenant, thrown down your altars, and killed your prophets with the sword. I alone am left, and they are seeking my life, to take it away."

He said, "Go out and stand on the mountain before the LORD, for the LORD is about to pass by." Now there was a great wind, so strong that it was splitting mountains and breaking rocks in pieces before the LORD, but the LORD was not in the wind; and after the wind an earthquake, but the LORD was not in the earthquake; and after the earthquake a fire, but the LORD was not in the fire; and after the fire a sound of sheer silence.

When Elijah heard it, he wrapped his face in his mantle and went out and stood at the entrance of the cave.

Then there came a voice to him that said, "What are you doing here, Elijah?" He answered, "I have been very zealous for the LORD, the God of hosts; for the Israelites have forsaken your covenant, thrown down your altars, and killed your prophets with the sword. I alone am left, and they are seeking my life, to take it away." Then the LORD said to him, "Go, return on your way to the wilderness of Damascus; when you arrive, you shall anoint Hazael as king over Aram. Also you shall anoint Jehu, son of Nimshi, as king of Israel; and Elisha, son of Shaphat of Abel-meholah, as prophet in your place. Whoever escapes from the sword of Hazael, Jehu shall kill; and whoever escapes from the sword of Jehu, Elisha shall kill. Yet I will leave seven thousand in Israel, all the knees that have not bowed to Baal, and every mouth that has not kissed him."

1 Kings 19:1-16

REFLECTION

When we think of hunger, we usually think of food. But hunger for food is only one of many hungers that people share. We hunger for love—to give it and to receive it. We hunger to touch others and to be touched—to shake hands, to be hugged, to be patted on the back. We hunger for the security of having a permanent home, a stable job, and a few possessions that bring comfort. And we hunger for someone to trust—someone we can confide in, someone whose advice we can take, someone who will keep his or her word, someone who will do the work well and on time. These are but a few of our many hungers.

In this story, Elijah is hungry. Fleeing the angry Jezebel, he leaves the ordinary world, with its companionship, food, and drink, far behind. His escape becomes a pilgrimage to a sacred place: Horeb, the mountain where Moses saw God in a burning bush. On the way, Elijah hungers for food, and God satisfies him with a hearth cake and a jug of water delivered by the angel of the Lord. Because Elijah allows himself to be entertained by the angel, God feeds him not only with cake and water but also with strength—enough to walk for forty days and forty nights.

Once Elijah arrives on the mountain, God feeds him with God's word. First God asks him why he has come to Horeb. Elijah catalogs his woes. Then God commands Elijah to stand before him. The traditional manifestations of God's presence—wind, earthquake, and fire—are reduced to mere precursors of a mysterious "sound of sheer silence." Alone on a mountain, Elijah is fed with the divine presence itself. His only response is to cover his face.

But Elijah is still not full. While he has obeyed God's command in part, he has not yet re-accepted his prophetic call. So God asks him a second time why he has come to Horeb. Elijah repeats his complaint. This time God commissions Elijah to anoint two kings and a prophet. To Elijah's desire to resign his mission in the face of Israel's infidelity, God responds by naming his successor—Elisha. To Israel's violence, God responds with the swords of Hazael and Jehu. To Elijah's claim of isolation, God asserts that there remain thousands of faithful in the land. In other words, God feeds Elijah with renewed enthusiasm and a future.

What Elijah learns through the angel of the Lord is what we so often forget: God satisfies all our hungers. No person or thing can completely alleviate our hungers. Only God feeds us with food that strengthens us, with a word and a presence that renew our dedication to our mission, and with a future that will never end.

⊙EOITATION

> ➤ Make a list of ten of your hungers.

> ➤ For each hunger, identify who satisfies it to some degree.

> ➤ For each hunger, identify how God can satisfy it completely.

> ➤ Who was the "angel" who entertained you while you dreamed of how God can satisfy completely all your hungers?

pRAyER

[God] commanded the skies above,

and opened the doors of heaven;

he rained down on [Israel] manna to eat,

and gave them the grain of heaven.

Mortals ate of the bread of angels;

he sent them food in abundance.

And they ate and were well filled,

for he gave them what they craved.

Psalm 78:23-25, 29

God Repents

David was stricken to the heart because he had numbered the people. David said to the LORD, "I have sinned greatly in what I have done. But now, O LORD, I pray you, take away the guilt of your servant; for I have done very foolishly." When David rose in the morning, the word of the LORD came to the prophet Gad, David's seer, saying, "Go and say to David: Thus says the LORD: Three things I offer you; choose one of them, and I will do it to you." So Gad came to David and told him; he asked him, "Shall three years of famine come to you on your land? Or will you flee three months before your foes while they pursue you? Or shall there be three days' pestilence in your land? Now consider, and decide what answer I shall return to the one who sent me."

Then David said to Gad, "I am in great distress; let us fall into the hand of the LORD, for his mercy is great; but let me not fall into human hands."

So the LORD sent a pestilence on Israel from that morning until the appointed time; and seventy thousand of the people died, from Dan to Beer-sheba. But when the angel stretched out his hand toward Jerusalem to destroy it, the LORD relented the evil, and said to the angel who was bringing destruction among the people, "It is enough; now stay your hand." The angel of the LORD was then by the threshing floor of Araunah the Jebusite.

When David saw the angel who was destroying the people, he said to the LORD, "I alone have sinned, and I alone have done wickedly; but these sheep, what have they done? Let your hand, I pray, be against me and against my father's house."

2 Samuel 24:10-17

REFLECTION

David's sin is power hunger. In spite of his chief of staff's good advice, David insists on taking a census of the Israelites. Since the people belong to God and not to David, only God should know how many Israelites there are. God is Israel's true king. David recognizes this fact only after the census is completed.

God treats David like a child, offering him three choices of punishment for taking the census. David chooses the three days' pestilence, because he trusts that God's "mercy is great." God proves that he is indeed merciful by stopping the action of the destroying angel. In effect, God repents of God's action. God has mercy on the people and upon their human king, David, who entertained the angel of the Lord without meaning to.

Don't we often experience God's repentant mercy in our lives? How often have we deserved the full force of divine wrath only to receive mercy and forgiveness instead! And God's mercy, like his wrath, may be—and usually is—mediated through an angel. Think about the last time that your spouse and you or your best friend and you had a strong disagreement. Didn't both of you eventually mediate mercy and forgiveness to each other, functioning as messengers of God's mercy?

How often we, like David, try to grab power and influence for ourselves, to make ourselves look better than others! Maybe we stretched the truth about an incident at work in order to make ourselves look better than the boss or a colleague. Maybe we thought of ourselves as better than people who wear skin of a color different from our own. Maybe we tossed out a number—our weight, our income, our university degrees—around people we knew would feel diminished by comparison. Whatever our sin, God's mercy stayed the hand of the angel who should have punished us severely.

MEDITATION

> When have you most recently experienced God's repentant mercy in your life?

> Who was the "angel" you entertained?

PRAYER

Bless the LORD, O my soul,
    and all that is within me,
    bless his holy name.
Bless the LORD, O my soul,
    and do not forget all his benefits—
    who forgives all your iniquity,
    who heals all your diseases,
    who redeems your life from the Pit,
    who crowns you with steadfast love and mercy,
    who satisfies you with good as long as you live;
    so that your youth is renewed like the eagle's.

The LORD is merciful and gracious,
    slow to anger and abounding in steadfast love.
He will not always accuse,
    nor will he keep his anger forever.
He does not deal with us according to our sins,
    nor repay us according to our iniquities.
For as the heavens are high above the earth,
    so great is his steadfast love
    toward those who fear him;
as far as the east is from the west,
    so far he removes our transgressions from us.

The steadfast love of the LORD is from everlasting to everlasting
    on those who fear him,
and his righteousness to children's children,
    to those who keep his covenant
    and remember to do his commandments.

Psalm 103:1-5, 8-12, 17-18

THREE ANGELS

FOR

APRIL

God Intervenes

God Opens the Way

God Lives

God Intervenes

God tested Abraham. He said to him, "Abraham!" And he said, "Here I am." He said, "Take your son Isaac, whom you love, and go to the land of Moriah, and offer him there as a burnt offering on one of the mountains that I shall show you." So Abraham rose early in the morning, saddled his donkey, and took two of his young men with him, and his son Isaac; he cut the wood for the burnt offering, and set out and went to the place in the distance that God had shown him.

On the third day Abraham looked up and saw the place far away. Then Abraham said to his young men, "Stay here with the donkey; the boy and I will go over there; we will worship, and then we will come back to you." Abraham took the wood of the burnt offering and laid it on his son Isaac, and he himself carried the fire and the knife. So the two of them walked on together.

Isaac said to his father Abraham, "Father!" And he said, "Here I am, my son." He said, "The fire and the wood are here, but where is the lamb for a burnt offering?" Abraham said, "God himself will provide the lamb for a burnt offering, my son." So the two of them walked on together.

When they came to the place that God had shown him, Abraham built an altar there and laid the wood in order. He bound his son Isaac, and laid him on the altar, on top of the wood. Then Abraham reached out his hand and took the knife to kill his son. But the angel of the LORD called to him from heaven, and said, "Abraham, Abraham!" And he said, "Here I am." He said, "Do not lay your hand on the boy or do anything to him; for now I know that you fear God, since you have not withheld your son, your only son, from me." And Abraham looked up and saw a ram, caught in a thicket by its horns. Abraham went and took the ram and offered it up as a burnt offering instead of his son.

The angel of the LORD called to Abraham a second time from heaven, and said, "By myself I have sworn, says the LORD: Be-

cause you have done this, and have not withheld your son, your
only son, I will indeed bless you, and I will make your offspring
as numerous as the stars of heaven and as the sand that is on the
seashore. And your offspring shall possess the gate of their enemies, and by your offspring all the nations of the earth gain
blessing for themselves, because you have obeyed my voice."

Genesis 22:1-13, 15-18

Reflection

At one time or another most of us face problems that we
cannot solve on our own. Outside intervention is necessary or we
will be in big trouble. Schoolchildren may get into playground
fights that require intervention from a teacher, who will first
separate the combatants and then help them solve their problem in a
more constructive way. Married couples sometimes reach an
impasse that requires the help of a third party—a pastor or a
marriage counselor—who will listen and respond to both husband
and wife. Some individuals have drinking or drug problems that
they cannot admit until concerned family members and friends
intervene by confronting them and insisting on treatment.

In the familiar story of Abraham's willingness to sacrifice
Isaac, the angel of the Lord—God in disguise—intervenes to save
Isaac and to renew the promises God made to Abraham. The angel
also mediates God's acceptance and approval of Abraham's total
obedience, for Abraham has not withheld his only beloved son.

Three themes of the story especially deserve our attention.
First, *God's demands are absolute.* Abraham was undoubtedly
familiar with child sacrifice, for it was widely practiced in his part of
the world. The story-teller, however, does not suggest that he was
following some ancient ritual designed to avert divine wrath. To the
contrary, Abraham's willingness to sacrifice Isaac is a result of his
trust in and obedience to God. The patriarch is ready to do whatever God asks of him, even though the sacrifice of his son—besides
grieving him deeply—will fly in the face of the promise that he will
be the father of countless descendants.

Second, *God's will is inscrutable.* Abraham does not sit down
with God and demand a logical reason for this demand. He does not
call a family council and seek a consensus as to the most reasonable

course of action. The patriarch is not interested in knowing why God is asking him to perform this deed. Abraham simply trusts God. He entrusts his entire life and future to God.

Third, *God speaks the word "grace" to Abraham.* There is more going on in this story than meets the eye. We suspect this as soon as the narrator says "on the third day" (Genesis 22:4), because throughout the Bible "three" is a sign, a code word, for God's presence. *Grace* is God's action of sharing his presence, his very being, with people. Through grace, God's presence washes over people in abundant waves. It is God's grace that moves Abraham to listen to God's call in the first place. It is also God's grace that provides the sacrificial animal.

And there is still more grace in this story. Isaac's life is a gift of God's grace: He has been redeemed through the alternate sacrifice of a ram. According to Jewish law, the firstborn, who belongs to God, is saved through the blood of a sheep. It is easy to see why the early Fathers of the Church viewed Isaac as a type of Christ—he carried the wood (cross); he was willing to shed his blood, like the passover lamb; and he was redeemed, receiving a resurrected life of pure grace.

Grace overflows as God's angel intervenes and Abraham entertains the messenger, receiving once again the promise that his descendants will be numerous and will bless all nations.

MEDITATION

> What demand have you received from God recently?

> Did you follow it unquestioningly or did you scrutinize it?

> What grace did you receive as God's final word?

> Who was the "angel" you entertained?

PRAYER

Happy are those whose way is blameless,

    who walk in the law of the LORD

Happy are those who keep his decrees,

    who seek him with their whole heart,

    who also do no wrong,

    but walk in his ways.

You have commanded your precepts

    to be kept diligently.

O that my ways may be steadfast

    in keeping your statutes!

Then I shall not be put to shame,

    having my eyes fixed on all your commandments.

I will praise you with an upright heart,

    when I learn your righteous ordinances.

I will observe your statutes;

    do not utterly forsake me.

Psalm 119:1-8

God Opens The Way

The LORD said to Moses, " . . . Tell the Israelites to go forward. But you lift up your staff, and stretch out your hand over the sea and divide it, that the Israelites may go into the sea on dry ground. Then I will harden the hearts of the Egyptians so that they will go in after them; and so I will gain glory for myself over Pharaoh and all his army, his chariots, and his chariot drivers."

The angel of God who was going before the Israelite army moved and went behind them; and the pillar of cloud moved from in front of them and took its place behind them. It came between the army of Egypt and the army of Israel. And so the cloud was there with the darkness, and it lit up the night; one did not come near the other at night.

Then Moses stretched out his hand over the sea. The LORD drove the sea back by a strong east wind all night, and turned the sea into dry land; and the waters were divided. The Israelites went into the sea on dry ground, the waters forming a wall for them on their right and on their left.

The Egyptians pursued, and went into the sea after them, all of Pharaoh's horses, chariots, and chariot drivers went after them. At the morning watch the LORD in the pillar of fire and cloud looked down upon the Egyptian army, and threw the Egyptian army into panic. He clogged their chariot wheels so that they turned with difficulty. The Egyptians said, "Let us flee from the Israelites, for the LORD is fighting for them against Egypt."

Then the LORD said to Moses, "Stretch out your hand over the sea, so that the water may come back upon the Egyptians, upon their chariots and chariot drivers." So Moses stretched out his hand over the sea, and at dawn the sea returned to its normal depth. As the Egyptians fled before it, the LORD tossed the Egyptians into the sea. The waters returned and covered the chariots and the chariot drivers, the entire army of Pharaoh that had followed them into the sea; not one of them remained. But the

Israelites walked on dry ground through the sea, the waters forming a wall for them on their right and on their left.

Thus the LORD saved Israel on that day from the Egyptians.

Exodus 14:15-17, 19-30

REfLECTION

A sour relationship. A tyrannical boss. Lack of money. Loneliness. Addiction. Whatever our problem, we instinctively look for a solution. Sometimes we look for a way through the difficulty; sometimes, a way around it. Or we may try to run away from it or pretend it doesn't exist.

Moses and the Israelites faced a big problem. There seemed no way through it or around it, and they couldn't run away. The situation was clear: the Sea of Reeds was on one side of them, and the Pharaoh's army on the other. Soon they would be totally exterminated at the hand of the always-changing-his-mind Pharaoh.

Moses needed a solution, and he needed it fast. God had brought the people to this point. Would he abandon them now? If Moses had any doubts, they were removed when the angel of the Lord moved into place between the Israelites and the Egyptians.

When the Israelites were trapped, God opened the way forward. This story of God's deliverance became the pivot on which the whole history of Israel and of Christianity turns. Stories of creation and the patriarchs prepare for the exodus; stories of the monarchy, the captivity, and the return to Jerusalem look back on it; and stories about Jesus' ministry, death, and resurrection fulfill it. Why? Because the exodus is the decisive event of God opening the way for—saving—the chosen people.

The "great escape" seems to be a compilation of two stories. According to one account, Moses divides the sea with his staff and Israel walks through on dry ground, the waters forming a wall to their right and to their left. When Israel gets to the other side, Moses stretches out his hand and the waters flow over the Egyptian army, destroying it. In the other account, God drives back the sea with a wind long enough for the Israelites to cross through the sea-bed during the night. The sea returns to its usual flow in the morning.

No matter how the story is told, clearly the victory belongs to God alone. In other words, God—through the angel-messenger—shows Israel the way.

What God did in the past, God continues to do in the present. God opens the way for us. His messengers are always showing us the way out of a predicament. Should we abandon a stalled relationship or continue to work on it? Respond to the boss with renewed hard work or stand up to unjust demands? Learn to live on less or look for an opportunity to earn more? Look for a congenial group to join or invite lonely people to join us where we are? Ask for medical help or exercise our will-power?

If our eyes are open, God's angels will show us the way; and if "none of the above" seems the only answer, sometimes angel-messengers will open totally new ways we never thought possible.

Throughout every day, God leads us past the army of our enemies, through the sea of our problems. God doesn't eliminate the tough times; God simply shows us where it's safe to cross. God opens up a way out.

In the Gospel of John, Jesus tells his disciples, " . . . You know the way to the place where I am going."

Thomas, however, is not so sure. "Lord, we do not know where you are going. How can we know the way?" he asks.

Jesus responds, "I am the way, and the truth, and the life" (John 14:4-6).

Jesus reveals what we have thought all along—that God loves to show us the way. When we reach the other side of the sea, all we can do is praise God for saving us.

MEDITATION

➤ What problem have you recently faced and solved?

➤ How did God open up a way out?

➤ Who was the "angel" you entertained?

PRAYER

I will sing to the LORD, for he has triumphed gloriously;

    horse and rider he has thrown into the sea.

The LORD is my strength and my might,

    and he has become my salvation;

    this is my God, and I will praise him,

    my father's God, and I will exalt him.

At the blast of your nostrils the waters piled up,

    the floods stood up in a heap;

    the deeps congealed in the heart of the sea.

You blew with your wind, the sea covered them;

    they sank like lead in the mighty waters.

In your steadfast love you led the people whom you redeemed;

    you guided them by your strength to your holy abode.

Exodus 15:1-2, 8, 10, 13

God Lives

After the sabbath, as the first day of the week was dawning, Mary Magdalene and the other Mary went to see the tomb. And suddenly there was a great earthquake; for an angel of the Lord, descending from heaven, came and rolled back the stone and sat on it. His appearance was like lightning, and his clothing white as snow . . . .

The angel said to the women, "Do not be afraid; I know that you are looking for Jesus who was crucified. He is not here; for he has been raised, as he said. Come, see the place where he lay. Then go quickly and tell his disciples, 'He has been raised from the dead, and indeed he is going ahead of you to Galilee; there you will see him.' This is my message for you."

So they left the tomb quickly with fear and great joy, and ran to tell his disciples.

Matthew 28:1-3, 5-8

REFLECTION

It is an angel of the Lord who announces that God has raised Jesus from the dead. Since the angel is a manifestation of God, and since Jesus is the Son of God, it is accurate to say that God announces that God lives!

In Matthew's Gospel, the kingdom of God is an ever-present theme. Look how Matthew uses the earthquake story to add to the glory of the resurrection narrative. The earthquake preceding the angel's opening of the tomb recalls a similar earthquake that immediately followed Jesus' death (see Matthew 27:51-53). These earthquakes are signs of an *apocalyptic* motif: a revelation, a breaking forth, of a new kind of life.

Matthew is showing that Jesus' death is the way from death to life. The stone that blocked the tomb's entrance had been the victory monument of death. Once the angel rolled it back and sat down on it, it became a sign of victory over death. Matthew uses the

56

earthquakes, the stone, and God's messenger-angel to shout that God's kingdom is come, that God lives.

The angel's message—"He has been raised from the dead"—is an early Christian creedal formula, a standardized way to express faith. The women entertain the angel of the Lord, receive the announcement, and function as apostles to the apostles. In other words, they are sent to those who have been sent previously and who will be sent again (see Matthew 28:16-20).

God's messenger announces that God lives. If we stand back for a moment and scan our own life experiences, we might be surprised to see angels delivering this same message to us.

The earthquake of surgery rolled back the stone of death-dealing cancer, and we experienced the power of God living in our bodily tissues.

Or the stone of hatred was rolled away and we were able to see that the tomb of prejudice is empty. For the first time we could see that all people—no matter of what color or gender or level of intelligence—are created in God's image and are loved equally by him.

When we entertain the angel of the Lord, we are likely to be frightened by earthquakes and rolling stones, overjoyed by the message that God lives. Then, in our fear and great joy, we will run to tell others the good news.

MEDITATION

> When have you recently experienced an earthquake in your life?

> From what tomb was the stone rolled away?

> Where did you see God's life in a new way?

> To whom were you sent?

> Who was the "angel" you entertained?

PRAYER

You who live in the shelter of the Most High,

    who abide in the shadow of the Almighty,

    will say to the LORD, "My refuge and my fortress;

    my God, in whom I trust."

For he will deliver you from the snare of the fowler,

    and from the deadly pestilence;

    he will cover you with his pinions,

    and under his wings you will find refuge . . . .

No evil shall befall you,

    nor scourge come near your tent.

For he will command his angels concerning you

    to guard you in all your ways.

On their hands they will bear you up,

    so that you will not dash your foot against a stone.

Psalm 91:1-4, 10-12

THREE ANGELS

FOR

MAY

God Reigns

God Acts

God Frees

God Reigns

SCRIPTURE

The LORD said to Moses: . . . Have [the Israelites] make me a sanctuary, so that I may dwell among them. They shall make an ark of acacia wood . . . . You shall overlay it with pure gold, inside and outside you shall overlay it, and you shall make a molding of gold upon it all around.

Then you shall make a mercy seat of pure gold . . . . You shall make two cherubim of gold; you shall make them of hammered work, at the two ends of the mercy seat. Make one cherub at the one end, and one cherub at the other; of one piece with the mercy seat you shall make the cherubim at its two ends. The cherubim shall spread out their wings above, overshadowing the mercy seat with their wings. They shall face one to another; the faces of the cherubim shall be turned toward the mercy seat. You shall put the mercy seat on the top of the ark; and in the ark you shall put the covenant that I shall give you. There I will meet you, and from above the mercy seat, from between the two cherubim that are on the ark of the covenant, I will deliver to you all my commands for the Israelites.

Exodus 25:1, 8, 10-11, 17-22

REFLECTION

The word *reign* is related to the words *king* and *queen* (*rex* and *regina* in Latin); other related English words include *royal, regal,* and *regent.* Although reign is not used in this selection from the Book of Exodus, the word aptly describes God's relationship with the Israelites. God is the king who rules the people from his throne, the place where people make contact with God.

The ark was a box that served as a storage container for the two tablets of the law. In God's design for the ark, the cover was called the mercy seat, or sometimes the *propitiatory.* The mercy seat, with a cherub at each end, was God's throne—the place where God would contact the Israelites.

In the ancient world, *cherubim* (plural of *cherub*, a high-ranking angel that is not at all cute) were portrayed as composite creatures with the physical characteristics of animals and humans. Usually winged, they served as guardians of the monarch's throne. Most likely they looked like human-headed winged lions, precursors of contemporary representations of angels.

The cherubim were thought of as God's angelic bodyguards. Their special task was to guard holy places and objects, such as the ark of the covenant. Upon them rested the divine majesty. From the cherubim-throne God reigned over Israel, but not as royalty separated from those who were ruled. The throne was the meeting place of God and humans, through God's word mediated by Moses.

God reigned from the sanctuary of his tent, which was placed in the midst of the people's tents. God reigned as a leader, rescuer, and defender of the chosen people, for whom he showed a jealous love. The cherubim functioned as the visible manifestation of the invisible God. They were the medium of God, through Moses, to the people.

Though in modern times cherubim are not always depicted as human-headed, animal-winged beings, they continue to form a throne upon which God sits to reign. Prior to the Second Vatican Council, God was often pictured as an old man dressed in white, sporting a gray beard, and seated upon a huge chair that was suspended on the backs of human heads with wings—the cherubim. On the right side of God's throne was another chair in which sat a young Jesus Christ, while a dove (the Holy Spirit) hovered above.

Today the Church emphasizes God's throne as mercy seat or meeting place. God chooses to reign from the throne of human hearts. When we respect the dignity of every person and show reverent concern to every individual, we recognize that God reigns in everyone.

God may reveal his throne—the place of meeting—to be in the shade of a tree on a hot summer's day, beside a gurney in a crowded hospital emergency room, at a table for two in a noisy restaurant, around a conference table in a hotel's executive suite, in an apartment in an inner-city housing project. Cherubim-thrones are everywhere.

Meditation

> Where have you most recently discovered the cherubim-throne from which God reigns?

> Who was the "angel" you entertained?

Prayer

Give ear, O Shepherd of Israel,

    you who lead Joseph like a flock!

You who are enthroned upon the cherubim, shine forth . . . .

Stir up your might,

    and come to save us!

Restore us, O God;

    let your face shine, that we may be saved.

Psalm 80:1-3

God Acts

SCRIPTURE

Sing and rejoice, O daughter Zion! For lo, I will come and dwell in your midst, says the LORD. Many nations shall join themselves to the LORD on that day, and shall be my people; and I will dwell in your midst. And you shall know that the LORD of hosts has sent me to you. The LORD will inherit Judah as his portion in the holy land, and will again choose Jerusalem.

Be silent, all people, before the LORD; for he has roused himself from his holy dwelling.

Then [the angel who spoke with me] showed me the high priest Joshua standing before the angel of the LORD . . . . The angel said to those who were standing before him, "Take off his filthy clothes." And to him he said, "See, I have taken your guilt away from you, and I will clothe you with festal apparel." And I said, "Let them put a clean turban on his head." So they put a clean turban on his head and clothed him with the apparel; and the angel of the LORD was standing by.

Then the angel of the LORD assured Joshua, saying "Thus says the LORD of hosts: If you will walk in my ways and keep my requirements, then you shall rule my house and have charge of my courts, and I will give you the right of access among those who are standing here. Now listen, Joshua, high priest . . . . !"

The angel who talked with me came again, and wakened me, as one is wakened from sleep. He said to me, "What do you see?" And I said, "I see a lampstand all of gold, with a bowl on the top of it; there are seven lamps on it, with seven lips on each of the lamps that are on the top of it. And by it there are two olive trees, one on the right of the bowl and the other on its left."

I said to the angel who talked with me, "What are these, my lord?" Then the angel who talked with me answered me, "Do you not know what these are?" I said, No, my lord." He said to me, "This is the word of the LORD . . . . : Not by might, nor by

power, but by my spirit, says the LORD of hosts. What are you,
O great mountain? . . . . You shall become a plain."

Zechariah 2:10-13; 3:1, 4-8; 4:1-7

REFLECTION

Nouns (persons, places, or things) are easier to picture than verbs (actions or being). For example, when we were learning how to read, the teacher said, "Draw a cup," and we drew either a teacup or a mug. However, when the teacher instructed us, "Draw drinking from a cup," we had to slow down the action of drinking to a single frame and portray someone sipping tea from a cup or gulping coffee from a mug.

We easily draw mental pictures of a cedar tree, a squirrel, or a book. It is much more difficult to visualize bending in the wind, eating a nut, or reading a tome. In fact, to do this we have to freeze-frame the noun ("squirrel") in the process of doing the verb ("eating"). Astute grammarians will notice that I have not even succeeded in talking about verbs as pictures in this paragraph. In each case, I have changed the verb (i.e., "to drink") into a gerund ("drinking"), which is functionally a noun, before trying to make a picture of it.

Basically, we do the same thing with God! There is little doubt among Christians that God is always revealing himself to people—an action often referred to as *grace* or *angel*. Notice that the only way to picture God's ongoing activity is to take a static photograph of it—that is, to turn it into a noun. So *grace* is drawn as lines flowing from a dove hovering over a group of believers huddled together or as strokes radiating from the hands of the Virgin Mary (titled "Our Lady of Grace"). *Angel* is pictured as a bodiless head with wings or as a white-robed young man with feathered appendages attached to his shoulders.

Zechariah is an *apocalyptic* prophet. He believes in a powerful realm beyond our own where God rules and events on earth are orchestrated. He expects God to intervene through some cataclysmic event and make a decisive change in the course of history. He communicates his beliefs and expectations through powerful word pictures. Nevertheless, Zechariah does not understand his own visions because he does not understand how God acts.

For Zechariah to comprehend what he has seen, the angel has to interpret. The mediating angel is a sign that God has become remote from humans. People no longer hear or understand God's word. The prophet stands helplessly before the unfolding visions, not knowing what they mean until the angel speaks.

What the angel reveals to Zechariah is that, when the Hebrews return from their exile in Babylon, God also will return to Jerusalem to be with his chosen people. Zechariah watches as the angel speaks with Joshua, the high priest and representative of the people. The angel tells Joshua that God will restore the royal family and remove the guilt of the land. God accomplishes what God wants.

When we feel remote from God, we can trust that God has not moved away from us. As soon as we, like Zechariah, entertain angels, we realize that God is present and active in our midst. We can't capture God and draw him, as if he were a noun; but we can see his action in our world as his messengers interpret our experiences for us.

MEDITATION

> ➤ What experience has revealed God-in-action to you?

> ➤ Have you turned the action into a static picture?

> ➤ If so, what "angel" do you need to entertain in order to restore it to a continuing revelation?

PRAYER

O LORD, how manifold are your works!

In wisdom you have made them all;

    the earth is full of your creatures.

These all look to you

    to give them food in due season;

    when you give to them, they gather it up;

    when you open your hand,

    they are filled with good things.

When you hide your face, they are dismayed;

    when you take away their breath, they die

    and return to their dust.

When you send forth your spirit, they are created;

    and you renew the face of the ground.

May the glory of the LORD endure forever;

    may the LORD rejoice in his works.

Psalm 104:24, 27-31

God Frees

Now many signs and wonders were done among the people through the apostles. [The people] . . . even carried out the sick into the streets, and laid them on cots and mats, in order that Peter's shadow might fall on some of them as he came by. A great number of people would also gather from the towns around Jerusalem, bringing the sick and those tormented by unclean spirits, and they were all cured.

Then the high priest took action; he and all who were with him (that is, the sect of the Sadducees), being filled with jealousy, arrested the apostles and put them in the public prison. But during the night an angel of the Lord opened the prison doors, brought them out, and said, "Go, stand in the temple and tell the people the whole message about this life." When they heard this, they entered the temple at daybreak and went on with their teaching.

Acts 5:12, 15-21

REFLECTION

While most of us probably have not spent time inside a prison cell, we may have visited someone in jail or at least seen a prison on the evening news. The many locked and barred gates and doors, the high strands of razor-sharp curled barbed wire atop chain-linked fences, the watchtowers strategically placed at each corner of the enclosure—all contribute to letting the inmates know that they are locked in. They have lost their freedom.

Scripture pictures the human race as prisoners in desperate need of the freedom God offers. This freedom has many facets.

God frees us from the prison of *alienation*. Through the death and resurrection of Jesus, God's Son, we have been reconciled to God, set free from all our sins. In freedom we pledge obedience to discern God's will for us and then to do all that we can to incarnate God's will in our lives.

The angel-messengers of the Lord can also free us from the prison of *physical pain or illness*. Often God uses the help of medical specialists to bring healing; often God also responds to prayer. Sometimes, rather than curing the disease, God gives the person strength to endure it and even to use it for God's glory.

Sometimes angels free us from the prison of *fear*. God uses professional counselors to help us, especially if our fear began long ago when, for example, our parents divorced, or we were abused, or we had other problems that we never confronted.

Messengers of the Lord take our prayers for freedom and present them to God. That is why we can be confident that we are always heard.

Our freedom, however, is not a liberty to do whatever we want. God sets us free for a purpose. The angel set the apostles free so that they could continue their healing ministry and their preaching about Jesus.

This act of liberation is the first of three such events recorded in the Acts of the Apostles. In the second freedom story, King Herod arrests Peter. "When he had seized him, he put him in prison and handed him over to four squads of soldiers to guard him, intending to bring him out to the people after the Passover" (Acts 12:4).

Herod's intentions, however, were foiled. "The very night before Herod was going to bring him out, Peter, bound with two chains, was sleeping between two soldiers, while guards in front of the door were keeping watch over the prison. Suddenly an angel of the Lord appeared and a light shone in the cell. He tapped Peter on the side and woke him, saying, 'Get up quickly.' And the chains fell off his wrists. The angel said to him, 'Fasten your belt and put on your sandals.' He did so. Then he said to him, 'Wrap your cloak around you and follow me.' Peter went out and followed him; he did not realize that what was happening with the angel's help was real; he thought he was seeing a vision" (Acts 12:6-9).

The light of God's presence shone in Peter's cell, and God set Peter free—free to keep proclaiming God's salvation. Peter knew whom to thank for his rescue. He "came to himself and said, 'Now I am sure that the Lord has sent his angel and rescued me from the hands of Herod. . .'" (Acts 12:11). Later, Peter explained ". . . how the Lord had brought him out of the prison" (Acts 12:17).

In the third prison escape story in the Acts of the Apostles, no angel is mentioned, but there is an earthquake—another signifier of divine intervention. "About midnight Paul and Silas were praying and singing hymns to God, and the prisoners were listening to them. Suddenly there was an earthquake, so violent that the foundations of the prison were shaken; and immediately all the doors were opened and everyone's chains were unfastened" (Acts 16:25-26).

Once God had freed Paul and Silas, the jailer took them to his home, where ". . . he and his entire family were baptized without delay" (Acts 16:33). Thus God freed Paul and Silas to continue their mission of converting the Gentiles.

Through angels God continues to set people free. What is the result in the lives of individuals who have been freed? A stronger faith, to be sure, as well as a desire to spread the good news: God is present and active in the world, and all prison gates have been opened through the death and resurrection of God's Son, Jesus Christ.

MEDITATION

- ➤ From what jail has God recently released you?
- ➤ For what purpose were you freed from that prison?
- ➤ Who was the "angel" you entertained?

PRAYER

Contend, O LORD, with those who contend with me;

fight against those who fight against me!

Take hold of shield and buckler,

and rise up to help me!

Draw the spear and javelin

  against my pursuers;

  say to my soul,

"I am your salvation."

Let them be put to shame and dishonor

  who seek after my life.

Let them be turned back and confounded

  who devise evil against me.

Let them be like chaff before the wind,

  with the angel of the LORD driving them on.

Let their way be dark and slippery,

  with the angel of the LORD pursuing them.

Psalm 35:1-6

THREE ANGELS

FOR

JUNE

God Encompasses All

God Pours Out Mercy

God Converts

God Encompasses All

SCRIPTURE

The word of the LORD came to the priest Ezekiel . . . . ; and the hand of the LORD was on him . . . . As I looked, a stormy wind came out of the north: a great cloud with brightness around it and fire flashing forth continually, and in the middle of the fire, something like gleaming amber. In the middle of it was something like four living creatures. This was their appearance: they were of human form. Each had four faces, and each of them had four wings. Their legs were straight, and the soles of their feet were like the sole of a calf's foot; and they sparkled like burnished bronze. Under their wings on their four sides they had human hands.

As for the appearance of their faces: the four had the face of a human being, the face of a lion on the right side, the face of an ox on the left side, and the face of an eagle; such were their faces. Their wings were spread out above; each creature had two wings, each of which touched the wings of another, while two covered their bodies.

As I looked at the living creatures, I saw a wheel on the earth beside the living creatures, one for each of the four of them. When they moved, they moved in any of the four directions without veering as they moved. Their rims were tall and awesome, for the rims of all four were full of eyes all around. Over the heads of the living creatures there was something like a dome, shining like crystal, spread out above their heads. And above the dome over their heads there was something like a throne, in appearance like sapphire; and seated above the likeness of a throne was something that seemed like a human form. Upward from what appeared like the loins I saw something like gleaming amber, something that looked like fire enclosed all around; and downward from what looked like loins I saw something that looked like fire, and there was a splendor all around. Like the bow in a cloud on a rainy day, such was the appearance of the splendor all around. This was the appearance of the likeness of the glory of the LORD.

Ezekiel 1:3-8, 10-11, 15, 17-18, 22, 26-28

REFLECTION

Consciously or unconsciously, most people sometimes wonder, *Where is God?* The question implies a location, a place where people can find God. But God is not in any one place. God encompasses all. God is infinite and omnipresent. God touches all things. God is everywhere.

This is the message of Ezekiel's vision of the divine throne occupied by God and supported by the four living creatures, later identified as the cherubim (see Ezekiel 10:5). Ezekiel's vivid description of these creatures shows clear connections to the ark of the covenant and its protective cherubim. The point of the vision is that no matter where God's people are—in Jerusalem or in captivity in Babylon or scattered throughout the earth—God is with them, protecting them.

The author of the Book of Revelation, writing to early Christians who were being persecuted for their faith, records a similar vision of four living creatures surrounding God's throne: "Around the throne, and on each side of the throne, are four living creatures, full of eyes in front and behind: the first living creature like a lion, the second living creature like an ox, the third living creature with a face like a human face, and the fourth living creature like a flying eagle. And the four living creatures, each of them with six wings, are full of eyes all around and inside" (Revelation 4:6-8).

The eyes, representing knowledge, indicate God's universal knowledge, and the four living creatures stand for God's nobility (lion), strength (ox), wisdom (human face), and swiftness (eagle). Put simply, the message of Revelation is the same as that of Ezekiel: God is with God's people, wherever they are and whatever trials they face.

Ezekiel's vision uses a variety of signs to indicate that God is everywhere. The stormy wind, for example, itself a sign of the divine presence, comes from the north, God's mythical home. Likewise, the flashing fire of the lightning recalls the burning bush that signaled God's presence to Moses. The four living creatures bring to mind the two cherubim that guarded the ark of the covenant, God's dwelling place in the Jerusalem Temple. The wheels indicate a war chariot, suggesting God's presence in battle; while the eyes reveal God's all-seeing presence. Because Israel's cosmology pictured God as dwelling above the heavens, Ezekiel sees God above the earth, "like the bow in a cloud on a rainy day."

We no longer use many of these ancient images to point to God's all-encompassing presence. Angels are still manifestations of God's presence everywhere, but we are likely to perceive them through different signs: perhaps through a friend's faithfulness, a serendipitous ordering of events, beauty or terror in the natural world, a word of wisdom from Scripture.

However we experience our angels, we know what they are telling us: God is here, with us, now.

MEDITATION

➢ What particular sign or image reminds you of God's all-encompassing presence?

➢ When did you last encounter it?

➢ Who was the "angel" you entertained?

PRAYER

In my distress I called upon the LORD;

    to my God I cried for help.

From his temple he heard my voice,

    and my cry to him reached his ears.

Then the earth reeled and rocked;

    the foundations also of the mountains trembled

    and quaked, because he was angry.

Smoke went up from his nostrils,

    and devouring fire from his mouth;

    glowing coals flamed forth from him.

He bowed the heavens, and came down;

    thick darkness was under his feet.

He rode on a cherub, and flew;

he came swiftly upon the wings of the wind.

He made darkness his covering around him,

his canopy thick clouds dark with water.

Out of the brightness before him

there broke through his clouds

hailstones and coals of fire.

Psalm 18:6-12

God Pours Out Mercy

SCRIPTURE

The word of the LORD came to the prophet Zechariah . . . . and Zechariah said, In the night I saw a man riding on a red horse! He was standing among the myrtle trees in the glen; and behind him were red, sorrel, and white horses. Then I said, "What are these, my lord?" The angel who talked with me said to me, "I will show you what they are." So the man who was standing among the myrtle trees answered, "They are those whom the LORD has sent to patrol the earth." Then they spoke to the angel of the LORD who was standing among the myrtle trees, "We have patrolled the earth, and lo, the whole earth remains at peace."

Then the angel of the Lord said, "O LORD of hosts, how long will you withhold mercy for Jerusalem and the cities of Judah, with which you have been angry these seventy years?" Then the LORD replied with gracious and comforting words to the angel who talked with me. So the angel who talked with me said to me, Proclaim this message: Thus says the LORD of hosts; I am very jealous for Jerusalem and for Zion. And I am extremely angry with the nations that are at ease; for while I was only a little angry, they made the disaster worse. Therefore, thus says the LORD, I have returned to Jerusalem with compassion; my house shall be built in it, says the LORD of hosts, and the measuring line shall be stretched out over Jerusalem. Proclaim further: Thus says the LORD of hosts: My cities shall again overflow with prosperity; the LORD will again comfort Zion and again choose Jerusalem.

Zechariah 1:7-17

REFLECTION

A lawyer pleads for the court's mercy for her client, asking for life imprisonment rather than the death penalty. A child asks his parent to show mercy and give him the five-dollar bill even though he has not completed all the chores. The head of the local soup kitchen asks for a donation in order to show mercy to the poor, to help those in distress.

While people demonstrate mercy, God *is* mercy. That is the angel's message in the prophet Zechariah's vision. God blesses with divine favor the people he has chosen.

God's mercy takes the form of peace. Zechariah sees messengers announcing that all the world is at peace. The angel of the Lord promises God's mercy: God will restore Jerusalem and Judah after the almost-seventy-year exile in Babylon.

The four horsemen represent the four corners of the earth—that is, the entire planet—to which God's merciful peace has spread. The number four suggests that the patrol is complete: the entire earth is covered.

The author of the Book of Revelation uses Zechariah's four horsemen as the first four of seven seals broken open by the Lamb, Jesus. These four horsemen represent the destruction of one quarter of the earth. This, too, is an outpouring of God's mercy to God's people: God is merciful to his people by eliminating those who persecute them.

The first horse is white (Revelation 6:2), a sign of victory. The second horse is red (6:4), representing bloody war—the means of destroying those who oppose God's chosen people. Black is the color of the third horse (6:5). The color black was associated with death. The last horse is pale green (6:8). The color may signify fear or ill health, or the death and decay that accompany war.

The visions of the four horses may look violent to us today. For the Revelator and for Zechariah, however, these horses were signs of the vindication and victory of God's people. The messenger-angels announce the meaning of the horses: God's mercy is limitless. God, who *is* mercy, spreads compassion to the four corners of the earth.

CꙅΘΙΤΑΤΙΟΝ

> ➤ How has God poured out mercy on you?

> ➤ How have you shown mercy to others?

> ➤ Who was the "angel" you entertained?

PRAYER

O give thanks to the LORD, for he is good;

    his steadfast love endures forever!

Let Israel say,

    "His steadfast love endures forever."

Let the house of Aaron say,

    "His steadfast love endures forever."

Let those who fear the LORD say,

    "His steadfast love endures forever."

Out of my distress I called on the LORD;

    the LORD answered me and set me in a broad place.

With the LORD on my side I do not fear.

O give thanks to the LORD, for he is good;

    for his steadfast love endures forever.

Psalm 118:1-6, 29

God Converts

In Caesarea there was a man named Cornelius, a centurion of the Italian Cohort, as it was called. He was a devout man who feared God with all his household; he gave alms generously to the people and prayed constantly to God. One afternoon at about three o'clock he had a vision in which he clearly saw an angel of God coming in and saying to him, "Cornelius." He stared at him in terror and said, "What is it, Lord?" He answered, "Your prayers and your alms have ascended as a memorial before God. Now send men to Joppa for a certain Simon who is called Peter . . . ." When the angel who spoke to him had left, he called two of his slaves and a devout soldier from the ranks of those who served him, and after telling them everything, he sent them to Joppa.

[Peter] went with them, and some of the believers from Joppa accompanied him. The following day they came to Caesarea. Cornelius was expecting them and had called together his relatives and close friends. On Peter's arrival Cornelius met him, and falling at his feet, worshiped him. But Peter made him get up, saying, "Stand up; I am only a mortal."

Then Peter began to speak to them: "I truly understand that God shows no partiality, but in every nation anyone who fears him and does what is right is acceptable to him." While Peter was still speaking, the Holy Spirit fell upon all who heard the word. The circumcised believers who had come with Peter were astounded that the gift of the Holy Spirit had been poured out even on the Gentiles, for they heard them speaking in tongues and extolling God. Then Peter said, "Can anyone withhold the water for baptizing these people who have received the Holy Spirit just as we have?" So he ordered them to be baptized in the name of Jesus Christ.

Acts 10:1-5, 7-8, 23-26, 34-35, 44-48

Reflection

Conversion, we tend to think, is something we do. We convert the floppy disks of our computers from one format to another. We change—a synonym for *convert*—from one laundry soap or softener to another one. We liquidate—another synonym—some assets in order to purchase a new car or replace a broken household appliance.

The usual religious understanding of conversion is to leave one denomination of believers in order to join another one. We are mistaken, however, if we think we do the converting. According to the Acts of the Apostles, God converts through angels. This is the point of the story about Cornelius. An angel, not human beings, directs the action. The angel, not Cornelius, demands that Peter be called. The Holy Spirit, not Peter, shows that the Gentiles as well as the Jews are God's people. The conversion of Cornelius and his household is due to divine, not human, initiative.

How does the author of the Acts of the Apostles show that this conversion is due to God's action? He tells of a second Pentecost—this one for the Gentiles—to parallel the first Pentecost (see Acts 2:1-11), at which only Jews were present. No one mediates the Spirit's action; no one says the right words or performs the right rituals in order to invoke the Spirit's presence. The Holy Spirit comes as God's gift, God's doing, before baptism has even been discussed. As soon as Peter recognizes what God has done, he asks, "Can anyone withhold the water for baptizing these people who have received the Holy Spirit just as we have?" (Acts 10:47).

Once God has decided, the Holy Spirit is poured out, and the Church follows. In fact, Paul launches his mission to the Gentiles after Peter explains to the Jewish Christians in Jerusalem how the Holy Spirit fell upon the Gentiles and how God granted them ". . . the repentance that leads to life" (Acts 11:18).

The main character in the Cornelius story, then, is God. The divine will is set in motion by an angel of God. People have their part to play in God's plan of salvation for all, but it is God—working through his messengers—who inspires the moves and sets the course.

MEDITATION

> ➤ What was your most recent experience of God prompting you to change your life?

> ➤ What was your deepest experience of conversion?

> ➤ From what did you convert?

> ➤ Who was the "angel" you entertained?

PRAYER

O LORD, you have searched me and know me.

You know when I sit down and when I rise up;

you discern my thoughts from far away.

You search out my path and my lying down,

and are acquainted with all my ways.

Even before a word is on my tongue,

O LORD, you know it completely.

Where can I go from your spirit?

Or where can I flee from your presence?

For it was you who formed my inward parts;

you knit me together in my mother's womb.

How weighty to me are your thoughts, O God!

How vast is the sum of them!

I try to count them—they are more than the sand;

I come to the end—

I am still with you.

Psalm 139:1-4, 7, 13, 17-18

THREE ANGELS

FOR

JULY

God Purifies

God Reveals the Son

God Guides

God Purifies

SCRIPTURE

I saw the Lord sitting on a throne, high and lofty; and the hem of his robe filled the temple. Seraphs were in attendance above him; each had six wings: with two they covered their faces, with two they covered their feet, and with two they flew. And one called to another and said:

"Holy, holy, holy is the LORD of hosts;

the whole the earth is full of his glory!"

The pivots on the thresholds shook at the voices of those who called, and the house filled with smoke.

And I said, "Woe is me! I am lost, for I am a man of unclean lips, and I live among a people of unclean lips; yet my eyes have seen the King, the LORD of hosts!" Then one of the seraphs flew to me, holding a live coal that had been taken from the altar with a pair of tongs.

The seraph touched my mouth with it and said: "Now that this has touched your lips, your guilt has departed and your sin is blotted out." Then I heard the voice of the Lord saying, "Whom shall I send, and who will go for us?" And I said, "Here am I; send me!"

Isaiah 6:1-8

REFLECTION

Purity means freedom from moral fault or guilt. Of course no human being—other than Jesus Christ and his mother, Mary—has ever been perfectly pure. *Pure* is an adjective that describes God alone. *Purify*, however, can describe the activity by which God makes us like himself.

In the account of Isaiah's vision and his call to be God's prophet, Isaiah tells how God, through the seraph's ministry, purified him of his defilement. The means of purification was a burning coal—fire, which in the ancient world was used to purify and burn animal, cereal, and incense offerings on altars, as well as to purify precious metals.

The seraphs—literally, "the fiery, burning ones"—are angels, traditionally of the highest rank. This is the only place in the Bible that mentions these mysterious creatures, each with six wings, a face, feet, and hands.

Most likely it is because of Isaiah's description of the winged seraphs that artists have portrayed all angels with wings. However, these seraphs are different from the angels we have met so far. They are not just God's messengers. Rather, they are part of the message. Their purpose is to fly around the throne on which God sits, singing his praises as they call attention to God's holiness, glory, and majesty.

Their cry most likely reflects the liturgy of the Jerusalem Temple. The glory of the transcendent God fills the earth. God rules over the whole world. God's holiness is so awesome that, out of reverence, the seraphs use two of their wings to cover their faces and two to cover their feet.

Isaiah does not say that the seraphs have hands, but hands are implied when a seraph takes an ember and places it against the prophet's lips, a gesture of purification. Thus the seraph serves as an agent of purification for Isaiah as he begins his prophetic ministry.

This event is a *theophany*, a manifestation of God's presence. The shaking door frame, the dense smoke, and the fiery ember from the altar recall God's appearance on Mount Sinai (see Exodus 19:16-19). Isaiah, insofar as a human being is able, sees God as the King of all the earth. Having seen God, he expects to die, for no one can see God and live (see Exodus 33:20; Judges 13:22). But instead of killing Isaiah, the seraph takes the burning coal and purifies him. God makes Isaiah worthy of the vocation to which God is calling him.

Now Isaiah becomes God's messenger. God asks, "Who will go for us?" It is as if a session of God's heavenly council has just ended and a messenger is needed to carry the news of the decision. The newly purified Isaiah immediately responds to the Lord's question by volunteering to be the prophetic messenger. "Here am I; send me!" he exclaims.

meditation

> ➤ In what ways has God purified you, enabling you to volunteer to be God's messenger?

> ➤ What was the instrument or sign of your purification?

> ➤ Who was the "angel" you entertained?

prayer

The LORD is king; let the peoples tremble!

He sits enthroned upon the cherubim; let the earth quake.

The LORD is great in Zion;

    he is exalted over all the peoples.

Let them praise your great and awesome name.

Holy is he!

Mighty King, lover of justice,

    you have established equity;

    you have executed justice

    and righteousness in Jacob.

Extol the LORD, our God;

    worship at his footstool.

Holy is he!

Psalm 99:1-5

God Reveals the Son

SCRIPTURE

The next day Jesus decided to go to Galilee. He found Philip and said to him, "Follow me." Now Philip was from Bethsaida, the city of Andrew and Peter. Philip found Nathanael and said to him, "We have found him about whom Moses in the law and also the prophets wrote, Jesus son of Joseph from Nazareth." Nathanael said to him, "Can anything good come out of Nazareth?" Philip said to him, "Come and see."

When Jesus saw Nathanael coming toward him, he said of him, "Here is truly an Israelite in whom there is no deceit." Nathanael asked him, "Where did you get to know me?" Jesus answered, "I saw you under the fig tree before Philip called you." Nathanael replied, "Rabbi, you are the Son of God! You are the King of Israel."

Jesus answered, "Do you believe because I told you that I saw you under the fig tree? You will see greater things than these." And he said to him, "Very truly, I tell you, you will see heaven opened and the angels of God ascending and descending upon the Son of Man."

John 1:43-51

REFLECTION

God is the source of all revelation. The author of John's Gospel makes it clear that Jesus did not reveal himself as God's Son; rather, God himself revealed his Son to the world. The story about the call of Philip and Nathanael is one instance of God's revelation of his Son.

Jesus calls Philip to follow him. Philip believes, responds, and in turn calls Nathanael, telling Nathanael that God has revealed Jesus through Moses and the prophets.

Nathanael responds with cynicism. How could Jesus come from God if he also comes from Nazareth, a town proverbial for its wickedness? But, unlike later cynics who would reject Jesus because of his origins or because of their reading of the law and the prophets, Nathanael responds to Philip's invitation and goes with him to find Jesus.

To understand what happens next, it helps to be familiar with stories about Jacob from the Book of Genesis. The patriarch Jacob had a reputation for dishonest dealing. When God converted Jacob ("supplanter"), he changed his name to Israel ("overcomer").

Nathanael is like Israel, says Jesus. He comes to God's revelation of the Son with an openness like that of the ancient patriarch, who willingly contended with a divine being and saw God (see Genesis 32:25-31). But Nathanael is not like Jacob, who deceived his brother Esau in order to steal his birthright and blessing. By contrast, Nathanael is a son of Israel in whom there is no deceit.

The honest Nathanael hears and accepts God's revelation of the Son. We know this through the names he uses for Jesus. First, Nathanael addresses Jesus as "Rabbi," or Teacher. Second, he calls Jesus the "Son of God" and the "King of Israel," two interrelated titles. In the Hebrew Bible, the king is often referred to as "son of God" (see, for example, 2 Samuel 7:14). Both terms were used for the expected Messiah.

After Nathanael receives the divine revelation, Jesus promises him that he will see greater things; he will receive more revelation about God's Son. Like Jacob, Nathanael will see God's messengers ascending and descending—not on a ladder, but "upon the Son of Man." John thus transforms Jacob's vision into a revelation of Jesus. Jesus is God's ladder from earth to heaven; Jesus is the pathway for God's self-revelation.

When Jesus calls himself the Son of Man, he acknowledges that he is the Messiah, the king who will redeem Israel. The term alludes to the prophet Daniel's vision of . . .

one like a human being [son of man]

coming with the clouds of heaven.

And he came to the Ancient One

and was presented before him.

To him was given dominion

and glory and kingship,

that all peoples, nations, and languages

should serve him.

His dominion is an everlasting dominion

that shall not pass away,

and his kingship is one

that shall never be destroyed.

Daniel 7:13-14

The story of Nathanael's call and response to God's revelation of the Son reminds us of God's call to each of us. Through the Scriptures, through preachers of the word, through other people, through nature, and through ordinary events, God continues to reveal the Son.

God invites us to respond to that revelation. If we, like Nathanael, answer God's call, we too will see the angels of God ascending and descending on Jesus, God's ladder from earth to heaven.

MEDITATION

➢ What means has God used to reveal his Son to you?

➢ What has God revealed about the Son to you?

➢ Who was the "angel" you entertained?

PRAYER

O LORD God of hosts,

who is as mighty as you, O LORD?

Your faithfulness surrounds you.

. . . You spoke in a vision to your faithful one and said:

"I have set the crown on one who is mighty,

I have exalted one chosen from the people.

I have found my servant, David;

with my holy oil I have anointed him;

hand shall always remain with him;

my arm also shall strengthen him.

He shall cry to me, 'You are my Father,

my God, and the Rock of my salvation!'

I will make him the first-born,

the highest of the kings of the earth.

Forever I will keep my steadfast love for him,

and my covenant with him will stand firm.

I will establish his line forever,

and his throne as long as the heavens endure."

Psalm 89:8, 19-21, 26-29

God Guides

An angel of the Lord said to Philip, "Get up and go toward the south to the road that goes down from Jerusalem to Gaza." (This is a wilderness road.) So he got up and went.

Now there was an Ethiopian eunuch, a court official of the Candace, queen of the Ethiopians, in charge of her entire treasury. He had come to Jerusalem to worship and was returning home; seated in his chariot, he was reading the prophet Isaiah. Then the Spirit said to Philip, "Go over to this chariot and join it." So Philip ran up to it and heard him reading the prophet Isaiah.

He asked, "Do you understand what you are reading?" He replied, "How can I, unless someone guides me?" And he invited Philip to get in and sit beside him.

Then Philip began to speak, and . . . he proclaimed to him the good news about Jesus. As they were going along the road, they came to some water; and the eunuch said, "Look, here is water! What is to prevent me from being baptized?" He commanded the chariot to stop, and both of them, Philip and the eunuch, went down into the water, and Philip baptized him. When they came out of the water, the Spirit of the Lord snatched Philip away; the eunuch saw him no more, and went on his way rejoicing.

Acts 8:26-31, 35-36, 38-39

REFLECTION

Most people who travel in foreign countries are happy to have a guide, someone who points out the sights, explains the history and culture, and interprets for them in stores and offices. Guides also offer their services in historic churches and museums, giving information about the edifice and various artifacts in the collection. Guidebooks and maps keep us from getting lost in strange cities and buildings, indicate where we should stop, and help us decide what to spend our time viewing.

God is a guide. God guides through angels and the Holy Spirit. In the story about Philip and the Ethiopian eunuch, God's guiding is referred to as "an angel of the Lord," "the Spirit," and "the Spirit of the Lord." God initiates the mission; Philip is a pawn to be used in the Spirit's strategy.

Through God's angel or Spirit, God guides Philip to where he wants him to be, enables him to proclaim Jesus to the eunuch, and makes it possible for him to baptize the first Gentile convert mentioned in the Acts of the Apostles. Guided by God, the gospel—the good news of Jesus—is moving toward the ends of the earth.

Just as God, through an angel or the Spirit, guided Philip to the eunuch, so God continues to guide people through messengers today.

When we have struggled through anxious days and sleepless nights with a problem seemingly too big to solve and then in a flash realized what we should do, God was guiding us to that decision.

When we have found ourselves talking with a stranger in a grocery store or at a rest stop along the interstate and then felt our hearts burning with God's love, the Spirit was leading us to that person for that moment of divine sharing.

When we have intuited that we had to be somewhere or do something and then had a new and unexpected experience that stretched us mentally, physically, or spiritually, God was sending us a message.

It is interesting to note that encounters with angels never last long. As soon as the message is delivered or the deed done or the experience finished, the messenger seems to disappear. Philip was snatched away, and "the eunuch saw him no more." The person who helped us make a decision, the stranger with whom we shared a moment, the intuition that led us to a new experience are gone in a flash. All we, like the eunuch, can do is go on our way rejoicing that God has, once again, guided us to where God wants us to be.

We can be sure there will be more messengers in the future. God never ceases to guide us. Who knows? God may even send us to others as a messenger of the good news about Jesus.

MEDITATION

> In what ways have you experienced God guiding you through a messenger?

> Who was the "angel" you entertained?

> In what ways have you been sent by God to another as a messenger, as Philip was sent to the eunuch?

> Who was the "angel" who sent you?

PRAYER

To you, O LORD, I lift up my soul.

O my God, in you I trust . . . .

Make me to know your ways, O LORD;

    teach me your paths.

Lead me in your truth, and teach me,

    for you are the God of my salvation;

    for you I wait all day long.

Good and upright is the LORD;

    therefore he instructs sinners in the way.

He leads the humble in what is right,

    and teaches the humble his way.

Psalm 25:1-2, 4-5, 8-9

THREE ANGELS

FOR

AUGUST

God Restores

God Deserves Worship

God Delivers the Law

God Restores

There was a festival of the Jews, and Jesus went up to Jerusalem. Now in Jerusalem by the Sheep Gate there is a pool, called in Hebrew Bethzatha, which has five porticoes. In these lay many invalids—blind, lame, and paralyzed. One man was there who had been ill for thirty-eight years. When Jesus saw him lying there and knew that he had been there a long time, he said to him, "Do you want to be made well?" The sick man answered him, "Sir, I have no one to put me into the pool when the water is stirred up; and while I am making my way, someone else steps down ahead of me." Jesus said to him, "Stand up, take up your mat and walk." At once the man was made well, and he took up his mat and began to walk.

Now that day was a sabbath. So the Jews said to the man who had been cured, "It is the sabbath; it is not lawful for you to carry your mat." But he answered them, "The man who made me well said to me, 'Take up your mat and walk.'" They asked him, "Who is the man who said to you, 'Take it up and walk'?" Now the man who had been healed did not know who it was, for Jesus had disappeared in the crowd that was there.

Later Jesus found him in the temple and said to him, "See, you have been made well! Do not sin any more, so that nothing worse happens to you." The man went away and told the Jews that it was Jesus who had made him well. Therefore the Jews started persecuting Jesus, because he was doing such things on the sabbath. But Jesus answered them, "My Father is still working, and I also am working." For this reason the Jews were seeking all the more to kill him, because he was not only breaking the sabbath, but was also calling God his own Father, thereby making himself equal to God.

John 5:1-3, 5-18

REFLECTION

Conspicuously absent from this scriptural account of Jesus' restoring the man who had been sick for thirty-eight years is the mention of an angel. Also absent is verse four, which begins to appear in manuscripts toward the end of the second century in the West and among the fourth-century Greek Fathers. Here is the missing verse, which contains the missing angel: "For an angel of the Lord went down at certain seasons into the pool, and stirred up the water; whoever stepped in first after the stirring of the water was made well from whatever disease that person had" (John 5:4).

Why is this verse not included in most contemporary translations of Scripture? Partly because it is not found at all in the earliest Greek manuscripts of John's Gospel. Neither does it appear in the Vulgate as translated by St. Jerome into Latin from the original languages. Scholars also point out that the verse is characteristically non-Johannine.

But these facts do not negate the truth that God does restore people to health, often using angel-messengers to signal his activity. Most likely the reference to the angel was added to this passage in order to explain the movement of the water and the apparently uncontested fact that people who stepped into the water were being healed.

Jesus restored the sick man to health, and the religious authorities were incensed. They weren't upset because the man was now healthy. They were furious because Jesus had healed him on a sabbath, thus breaking the law against work on the seventh day. They were even more furious because Jesus called God his Father, thus making himself equal to God. In their eyes, this was blasphemy of the worst sort.

Today God continues to upset the status quo by restoring people through messengers who stir up the water.

A person goes from door to door in the neighborhood, seeking signatures on a petition to city hall to get a park refurbished so children may play there in safety. The authorities, who have other ideas about how revenues should be used, are upset; but they cannot ignore the voice of the people. Playground equipment is installed, and volunteer vigilantes keep drug dealers at bay. An angel is stirring the water, and a neighborhood is being healed.

A group of Christians decide to open a halfway house for paroled prisoners, but the neighbors object. What will happen to property values? What about their families' personal safety? The proponents explain to the media, at public gatherings, in churches, what they are attempting to do. They show from past experience that public safety will not be endangered. They also introduce their neighbors to former criminals who are now responsible citizens thanks to similar programs in other towns. Permission for the halfway house is granted. An angel is stirring the water, and individuals are being rehabilitated.

Someone at work is treated unfairly. Because of this, someone else is promoted. You see the mistreated person's discouragement, and you go quietly to the boss. She doesn't want to listen; the situation threatens to be messy. Soon someone else goes to speak to her, and then others follow. Eventually she sees that ignoring the injustice will cause more problems than dealing with it. An angel is stirring the water, and justice is being restored.

Look around you and listen for the movement of the waters. You can be sure that an angel is at work, and that God is restoring someone to the fullness of life.

MEÒITATION

> What was your most profound experience of something or someone being restored by God?

> What water was stirred up?

> Who was the "angel" who did the stirring?

PRAYER

The LORD has done great things for us,
> and we rejoiced.

Restore our fortunes, O LORD,
> like the watercourses in the Negeb.

May those who sow in tears
> reap with shouts of joy.

Those who go out weeping,

    bearing the seed for sowing,

    shall come home with shouts of joy,

    carrying their sheaves.

Psalm 126:3-6

God Deserves Worship

SCRIPTURE

From the throne came a voice saying,

"Praise our God,

   all you his servants,

and all who fear him,

   small and great."

Then I heard what seemed to be the voice of a great multitude, like the sound of many waters or mighty thunderpeals, crying out,

"Hallelujah!

For the Lord our God

   the Almighty reigns.

Let us rejoice and exult

   and give him the glory,

for the marriage of the Lamb has come,

   and his bride has made herself ready;

to her it has been granted to be clothed

   with fine linen, bright and pure"—

for the fine linen is the righteous deeds of the saints.

And the angel said to me, "Write this: Blessed are those who are invited to the marriage supper of the Lamb." And he said to me, "These are true words of God." Then I fell down at his feet to worship him, but he said to me, "You must not do that! I am a fellow servant with you and your comrades who hold the testimony of Jesus. Worship God! For the testimony of Jesus is the spirit of prophecy."

Revelation 19:5-10

REfLECTION

People have always found it hard to keep their worship centered on God. For many people today, money is their primary object of worship. Their sacraments are celebrated with the things money can buy.

Look at the typical family room. The furniture is arranged in a semicircle around the household shrine, a cabinet-tabernacle whose doors open to reveal a large-screen television set.

Television helps create a hunger for other objects of worship: clothes, perfume, houses, pools, golf courses, real estate, stocks and bonds, luxurious cars, fine food and wine. Our worship of such "foreign gods" is usually not intended. We just slip into it, as into a deep sleep.

John the Revelator came close to worshiping someone who was not God. He had heard the heavenly music and seen the sacred vision, and when he saw the angel he "fell down at his feet to worship him." The angel immediately stopped him. "Worship God!" he said.

Why is God alone worthy of our worship? Because every good thing we have is a gift from God. God, through Christ ("the Lamb"), has married his faithful servant-community ("his bride") and endowed her with all heavenly blessings. God's reign, sealed with solemn covenant promises (like marriage vows), has begun.

The angel tells John that even the angelic messenger is a fellow servant with human beings—that is, part of God's gift. Worship focuses not on the gift but on the Giver. All rejoicing and celebrating and wedding feasting are to be directed toward God, who alone deserves all praise.

With the vision of the heavenly marriage lingering in our minds, we are reminded that we, along with the angel, "hold the testimony of Jesus." In other words, we are witnesses—people who know the truth about Jesus from first-hand experience and from God's word; people who are willing to tell the truth, whatever it may cost; people who put our integrity on the line for what we believe. This is one way we give praise and worship to God.

It is easy to slip into the worship of created things rather than that of God, the Creator. However, when we make the testimony of Jesus first in our life—when our lives witness to the word of God—nothing can get in the way of our worship. But if we seem to be in danger of forgetting this, an angel is always willing to remind us.

(DEDITATION

> ➤ Honestly, what things do you worship?

> ➤ When have you been a faithful witness to the word of God—that is, truly lived it?

> ➤ Who was the "angel" who led you to true worship?

PRAYER

Holy, holy, holy

　　the Lord God the Almighty,

　　　who was and is and is to come.

You are worthy, our Lord and God,

　　to receive glory and honor and power,

　　for you created all things,

　　and by your will they existed

　　and were created.

Worthy is the Lamb that was slaughtered

　　to receive power and wealth and wisdom and might

　　and honor and glory and blessing!

Hallelujah!

Salvation and glory and power to our God,

　　for his judgments are true and just . . . .

Amen. Hallelujah!

Revelation 4:8, 11; 5:12; 19:1-2, 4

God Delivers the Law

SCRIPTURE

[Stephen said,] "Now when forty years had passed, an angel appeared to [Moses] in the wilderness of Mount Sinai, in the flame of a burning bush. When Moses saw it, he was amazed at the sight; and as he approached to look, there came the voice of the Lord: 'I am the God of your ancestors, the God of Abraham, Isaac, and Jacob.' Moses began to tremble and did not dare to look.

"Then the Lord said to him, 'Take off the sandals from your feet, for the place where you are standing is holy ground. I have surely seen the mistreatment of my people who are in Egypt and have heard their groaning, and I have come down to rescue them. Come now, I will send you to Egypt.'

"It was this Moses whom they had rejected when they said, 'Who made you a ruler and a judge?' and whom God now sent as both ruler and liberator through the angel who appeared to him in the bush. He led them out, having performed wonders and signs in Egypt, at the Red Sea, and in the wilderness for forty years.

"This is the Moses who said to the Israelites, 'God will raise up a prophet for you from your own people as he raised me up.' He is the one who was in the congregation in the wilderness with the angel who spoke to him at Mount Sinai, and with our ancestors; and he received living oracles to give us . . . .

"You are the ones that received the law as ordained by angels, and yet you have not kept it."

Acts 7:30-38, 53

REFLECTION

We humans try to protect ourselves through laws. Family rules about curfew, eating between meals, and speaking politely become "laws." Clubs, homeowners' associations, and labor unions often have a constitution and a set of by-laws. Government—federal, state, county, and local—operates according to laws passed by legislatures and councils. The Church makes decisions based on a body of ecclesiastical law known as Canon Law.

Underneath and above our human laws is God's law—Torah, spelled out in the five Books of Moses and summarized in the Ten Commandments. In the lengthy homily Stephen gave just before he was martyred, he talks about God's law.

Stephen associates angels with the giving of the law. He is not alone in doing this. In his Letter to the Galatians, Paul says that the law "was ordained through angels by a mediator" (Galatians 3:19). Likewise, the author of the Letter to the Hebrews refers to "the message declared through angels" (Hebrews 2:2).

The Jews of Stephen's day thought they were giving glory to God by saying the law was delivered by angels. They did not want to involve the transcendent God in anything as messy as human situations. Stephen, Paul, and the author of the Book of Hebrews had a different perspective. In their eyes, the law given by Christ— God's Son—is superior to the law given by Moses and the angels, because Christ is superior to angels and humans.

What is Christ's law? It is, simply, love of God and love of neighbor. This law is first found in the Pentateuch (see Deuteronomy 6:5; Leviticus 19:18); it succinctly states the principle behind every law of Moses. Ideally, it is the foundation of our city, state, and national laws. Certainly it should be the foundation of our family laws.

Laws, when enacted and obeyed in love, protect people. Whenever people are writing laws that promote justice, wherever people are living by God's law of love, an angel-messenger is probably guiding them.

ᙏEᙁITᙁTIOᙁ

➤ What do you think is the best law ever written by your town, city, state, nation?

➤ What law do you take great pleasure in keeping?

➤ What "law" have you been involved in developing?

➤ While doing so, who was the "angel" you entertained?

PRAYER

Deal bountifully with your servant,

    so that I may live and observe your word.

Open my eyes, so that I may behold

    wondrous things out of your law.

I live as an alien in the land;

    do not hide your commandments from me.

My soul is consumed with longing

    for your ordinances at all times.

Your decrees are my delight;

    they are my counselors.

Psalm 119:17-20, 24

THREE ANGELS

FOR

SEPTEMBER

Who Is Like God?

God Strengthens

God Heals

Who Is Like God?

SCRIPTURE

War broke out in heaven; Michael and his angels fought against the dragon. The dragon and his angels fought back, but they were defeated, and there was no longer any place for them in heaven. The great dragon was thrown down, that ancient serpent, who is called the Devil and Satan, the deceiver of the whole world—he was thrown down to the earth, and his angels were thrown down with him.

Then I heard a loud voice in heaven, proclaiming,

"Now have come the salvation and the power

and the kingdom of our God

and the authority of his Messiah,

for the accuser of our comrades has been thrown down,

who accuses them day and night before our God.

But they have conquered him by the blood of the Lamb

and by the word of their testimony,

for they did not cling to life even in the face of death.

Rejoice then, you heavens,

and those who dwell in them!"

Revelation 12:7-12

REFLECTION

On September 29 the Roman Catholic Church celebrates the Feast of Michael, Gabriel, and Raphael, Archangels. Until the reform of the liturgical calendar in 1970, when Pope Paul VI established one feast day for all three archangels together, each had his own memorial (Michael, May 8 and September 29; Gabriel, March 24; and Raphael, October 24). We shall entertain Gabriel and Raphael later, but for now we focus on Michael.

Michael's name means "Who is like God?" He first appears in the Book of the Prophet Daniel, in which he is portrayed as Israel's guardian angel. An angel comes to Daniel in a vision and tells him why it has taken some time for God to answer his prayer for Israel's liberation from her enemies (see Daniel 10:1-11:2). The angel says, "The prince of the kingdom of Persia opposed me twenty-one days. So Michael, one of the chief princes, came to help me, and I left him there with the prince of the kingdom of Persia, and have come to help you understand what is to happen to your people at the end of days" (Daniel 10:12-14). Later the messenger says, "There is no one with me who contends against these princes except Michael, your prince" (Daniel 10:21).

The Jews had long believed that every nation has its guardian angel (see Deuteronomy 32:8). As Israel's guardian, Michael is one of the chief princes or archangels. Daniel makes this clear at the end of his series of revelations: "At that time Michael, the great prince, the protector of your people, shall arise" (Daniel 12:1).

When the author of the Book of Revelation writes about Michael's defeat of the dragon, he has Daniel's vision in mind. The archangel continues to guard God's people, now protecting them from evil. Christians are acquitted in the heavenly court because of Jesus' death. Their vindication in heaven reverses their condemnation on earth, where they are executed because of their faith.

Michael is mentioned in the Bible only one other time, in the New Testament Letter of Jude. An apocryphal book, The Assumption of Moses, deals with Moses' death and his assumption into heaven after a struggle between Michael and Satan for his body. The ninth verse of Jude refers to this legend.

Jude cautions his readers not to revile angelic beings. He writes, "When the archangel Michael contended with the devil and disputed about the body of Moses, he did not dare to bring a condemnation of slander against him, but said, 'The Lord rebuke you!'" (Jude 9). If the archangel refrained from speaking evil of the devil, Jude admonishes, how much worse it is for mere humans to revile angels.

Now that we have located Michael in the Bible, how might we entertain him? A clue is contained in the meaning of his name—"Who is like God?" Pope Gregory the Great once wrote that some angels are given proper names to denote the service they are empowered to perform. Whenever some act of wondrous power must be performed,

Gregory explained, Michael is sent, so that by his action and by his name he may proclaim that no one can do what God does by his superior power. Who, then, is like God? No one, Michael proclaims by his very name.

All too often we want supreme power for ourselves. In school we learn the ropes quickly. We discover who has the power and how we can manipulate it to our advantage. On the job we begin at the bottom of the corporate ladder and work our way up to a more powerful position. We refer to our country as the last superpower. Even in our families, members struggle for the front seat in the car, the first place in line, the place at the head of the table. Always we are grasping for more power.

Although we are created in the image and likeness of God, we are not God. We are human beings. God alone is all-powerful. Through Michael, God defeats evil, guards people, and proclaims that only God possesses supreme power. Through Michael, God reminds us that no one is like God.

MEDITATION

➤ What was your latest attempt to seize power of any kind?

➤ How were you reminded that all power belongs only to God?

➤ Who was the "archangel" who reminded you?

PRAYER

The earth is the LORD's and all that is in it,

>   the world, and those who live in it . . . .

Lift up your heads, O gates!

>   and be lifted up, O ancient doors!

>   that the King of glory may come in.

Who is the King of glory?

The LORD, strong and mighty,

>   the LORD, mighty in battle.

Lift up your heads, O gates!

    and be lifted up, O ancient doors!

    that the King of glory may come in!

Who is this King of glory?

The LORD of hosts,

    he is the King of glory.

God Strengthens

Once when [Zechariah] was serving as priest before God and his section was on duty, he was chosen by lot, according to the custom of the priesthood, to enter the sanctuary of the Lord and offer incense. Now at the time of the incense offering, the whole assembly of the people was praying outside. Then there appeared to him an angel of the Lord, standing at the right side of the altar of incense. When Zechariah saw him, he was terrified; and fear overwhelmed him.

But the angel said to him, "Do not be afraid, Zechariah, for your prayer has been heard. Your wife Elizabeth will bear you a son, and you will name him John. You will have joy and gladness, and many will rejoice at his birth, for he will be great in the sight of the Lord. He must never drink wine or strong drink; even before his birth he will be filled with the Holy Spirit. He will turn many of the people of Israel to the Lord their God. With the spirit and power of Elijah he will go before him, to turn the hearts of parents to their children, and the disobedient to the wisdom of the righteous, to make ready a people prepared for the Lord."

Zechariah said to the angel, "How will I know that this is so? For I am an old man, and my wife is getting on in years." The angel replied, "I am Gabriel. I stand in the presence of God, and I have been sent to speak to you and to bring you this good news. But now, because you did not believe my words, which will be fulfilled in their time, you will become mute, unable to speak, until the day these things occur."

. . . The angel Gabriel was sent by God to a town in Galilee called Nazareth, to a virgin engaged to a man whose name was Joseph, of the house of David. The virgin's name was Mary. And he came to her and said, "Greetings, favored one! The Lord is with you." But she was much perplexed by his words and pondered what sort of greeting this might be. The angel said to her, "Do not be afraid, Mary, for you have found favor with God. And now, you will conceive in your womb and bear a son, and you will name him Jesus. He will be great, and will be called the Son of the Most High, and the Lord God will give to him the throne of his ancestor David. He will reign over the house of Jacob forever, and of his kingdom there will be no end."

Mary said to the angel, "How can this be, since I am a virgin?" The angel said to her, "The Holy Spirit will come upon you, and the power of the Most High will overshadow you; therefore the child to be born will be holy; he will be called Son of God. And now, your relative Elizabeth in her old age has also conceived a son; and this is the sixth month for her who was said to be barren. For nothing will be impossible with God." Then Mary said, "Here am I, the servant of the Lord; let it be with me according to your word." Then the angel departed from her.

Luke 1:8-20, 26-38

REFLECTION

Gabriel, whose name means "God's strength," is not called an archangel in the Bible. That title comes from the apocryphal Book of Enoch, in which Gabriel is named as one of seven archangels. Like Michael, Gabriel makes his first biblical appearance in the Book of Daniel. There he explains to the prophet the meaning of the vision of the ram and the he-goat (see Daniel 8:1-14).

The author records, "When I, Daniel, had seen the vision, I tried to understand it. Then someone appeared standing before me, having the appearance of a man, and I heard a human voice . . . calling, 'Gabriel, help this man understand the vision.' So he came near where I stood; and when he came, I became frightened and fell prostrate. But he said to me, 'Understand, O mortal, that the vision is for the time of the end'" (Daniel 8:15-17).

The next time Gabriel appears to Daniel, he announces when God's people will be delivered from their Babylonian exile. The author writes, ". . . While I was speaking in prayer, the man Gabriel, whom I had seen before in a vision, came to me in swift flight at the time of the evening sacrifice" (Daniel 9:21). Gabriel tells Daniel that "an anointed one" will be the agent of God's deliverance.

Luke understands Gabriel's prophecy about an anointed one to refer to the Messiah, Jesus of Nazareth, the Anointed Son of God. In Luke's Gospel, Gabriel delivers messages of deliverance to both Zechariah and Mary. Zechariah's wife Elizabeth will conceive John the Baptizer, the herald of the Messiah; and Mary will conceive Jesus, "God saves," who will take David's throne and rule over the house of Jacob forever.

As we read Luke's account, we recognize the unity of God's plan of salvation: The same Gabriel who announced deliverance to Daniel also announces it to Zechariah and to Mary. Gabriel might be called a "liturgical angel" because in both Daniel and Luke he appears at the time of prayer and sacrifice. By evoking the atmosphere of Daniel's visions in his Gospel, Luke ties together Jesus' birth and Israel's messianic hopes.

In his *Homilies on the Gospels*, Pope Gregory the Great says that the word angel denotes a function rather than a nature. The holy spirits of heaven are called angels when they deliver messages. If the message is of supreme importance, they are called archangels. It is only fitting that the archangel Gabriel, "God's strength," should announce the greatest of all messages, the incarnation of the Messiah.

Whenever we experience the limitations of our own strength—physical, mental, emotional, or spiritual—we can also experience the opportunity to entertain an archangel and be strengthened by God, whose strength surpasses all human strengths combined. Wherever we see any type of human strength, most likely an archangel-messenger is present. Gabriel reminds us that our strength comes from God and is a manifestation of God's strength.

MEDITATION

> ➢ What are your strengths? Make a list.

> ➢ For each strength, ask: How does your strength remind you of God's strength?

> ➢ Who was the "archangel" you entertained?

PRAYER

I love you, O LORD, my strength.

The LORD is my rock, my fortress, and my deliverer,

    my God, my rock in whom I take refuge,

    my shield, and the horn of my salvation,

    my stronghold.

I call upon the LORD, who is worthy to be praised,

    so I am saved from my enemies.

For who is God except the LORD?

And who is a rock besides our God?—

    the God who girded me with strength,

    and made my way safe.

He made my feet like the feet of a deer,

    and set me secure on the heights.

The LORD lives! Blessed be my rock,

    and exalted be the God of my salvation.

Psalm 18:1-3, 31-33, 46

God Heals

Tobias went out to look for a man to go with him to Media, someone who was acquainted with the way. He went out and found the angel Raphael standing in front of him; but he did not perceive that he was an angel of God . . . .

. . . Then Tobias went out and called [Raphael], and said, "Young man, my father is calling for you." So he went in to him, and Tobit greeted him first. [Raphael] replied, "Joyous greetings to you!" But Tobit retorted, "What joy is left for me any more? I am a man without eyesight; I cannot see the light of heaven, but I lie in darkness. . . ." But the young man [Raphael] said, "Take courage; the time is near for God to heal you; take courage." Then Tobit said to him, "My son Tobias wishes to go to Media. Can you accompany him and guide him?" . . . He answered, "I can go with him, and I know all the roads, for I have often gone to Media and have crossed all its plains, and I am familiar with its mountains and all its roads." . . .

. . .The young man went out and the angel went with him; and the dog came out with him and went along with them. So they both journeyed along, and when the first night overtook them they camped by the Tigris river. Then the young man went down to wash his feet in the Tigris river. Suddenly a large fish leaped up from the water . . . and he cried out. But the angel said to the young man, "Catch hold of the fish and hang on to it!" So the young man grasped the fish and drew it up on the land. Then the angel said to him, "Cut open the fish and take out its gall, heart, and liver. Keep them with you, but throw away the intestines. For its gall, heart, and liver are useful as medicine.". . .

The two continued on their way together until they were near Media. Then the young man questioned the angel and said to him, "Brother Azariah, what medicinal value is there in the fish's heart and liver, and in the gall?" He replied, "As for the fish's heart and liver, you must burn them to make a smoke in the presence of a man or woman afflicted by a demon or evil spirit, and every affliction will flee away and never remain with that person any longer. And as for the gall, anoint a person's eyes where white films have appeared on them; blow upon them, upon the white films, and the eyes will be healed.". . .

When he entered Media . . . Raphael said to the young man, "Brother Tobias." "Here I am," he answered. Then Raphael said to him, "We must stay this night in the home of Raguel. He is your relative, and he has a daughter named Sarah. He has no male heir and no daughter except Sarah only, and you, as next of kin to her, have before all other men a hereditary claim on her."

Then Tobias said in answer to Raphael, "Brother Azariah, I have heard that she has already been married to seven husbands and that they died in the bridal chamber. On the night they went in to her, they would die. I have heard people saying that it was a demon that killed them.". . .

But Raphael said to him, " . . . Now listen to me, brother, and say no more about this demon. Take her. I know that this very night she will be given to you in marriage. When you enter the bridal chamber, take some of the fish's liver and heart, and put them on the embers of the incense. An odor will be given off; the demon will smell it and flee, and will never be seen near her any more.". . .

When they had finished eating and drinking, they wanted to retire; so they took the young man and brought him into the bedroom. Then Tobias remembered the words of Raphael, and he took the fish's liver and heart out of the bag where he had them and put them on the embers of the incense. The odor of the fish so repelled the demon that he fled to the remotest parts of Egypt. But Raphael followed him, and at once bound him there hand and foot . . . .

When they came near to Kaserin, which is opposite Nineveh, Raphael said, "You are aware of how we left your father. Let us run ahead of your wife and prepare the house while they are still on the way." As they went on together Raphael said to him, "Have the gall ready." And the dog went along behind them . . . .

Raphael said to Tobias, before he had approached his father, "I know that his eyes will be opened. Smear the gall of the fish on his eyes; the medicine will make the white films shrink and peel off from his eyes, and your father will regain his sight and see the light.". . .

. . .Then Tobit got up and came stumbling out through the courtyard door. Tobias went up to him, with the gall of the fish in his hand, and holding him firmly, he blew into his eyes, saying, "Take courage, father." With this he applied the medicine on his eyes, and it made them smart. Next, with both hands he peeled off the white films from the corners of his eyes. Then Tobit saw his son and threw his arms around him, and he wept and said to him, "I see you, my son, the light of my eyes!". . .

Then Raphael called the two of them privately and said to them: "Bless God and acknowledge him in the presence of all the living for the good things he has done for you. Bless and sing praise to his name. With fitting honor declare to all people the deeds of God. Do not be slow to acknowledge him . . . .

. . .God sent me to heal you and Sarah your daughter-in-law. I am Raphael, one of the seven angels who stand ready and enter before the glory of the Lord."

The two of them were shaken; they fell face down, for they were afraid. But he said to them, "Do not be afraid; peace be with you. Bless God forevermore. As for me, when I was with you, I was not acting on my own, but by the will of God. Bless him each and every day; sing his praises . . . . So now get up from the ground, and acknowledge God. See, I am ascending to him who sent me. Write down all these things that have happened to you." And he ascended. Then they stood up, and could see him no more. They kept blessing God and singing his praises, and they acknowledged God for these marvelous deeds of his, when an angel of God had appeared to them.

Tobit 5:4, 10; 6:1-5, 6-12, 14, 16-18; 8:1-3; 11:1-4, 7-8,
10-14; 12:6, 14-18, 20-22

REfLECTION

The name *Raphael,* "God's remedy" or "God heals," comes from the Hebrew *rapha,* "healer," "doctor," or "surgeon." This archangel appears in the Old Testament Book of Tobit and the apocryphal Book of Enoch, where he is portrayed as the concretization of God's healing power. In other words, Raphael is the messenger of God-as-healer. Furthermore, he protects travelers and defends people from the attacks of demons.

According to Pope Gregory the Great, the lesson to be learned from Raphael in the Book of Tobit is that God heals. When Raphael touches Tobit's eyes to cure him, he banishes the darkness of his blindness. Besides curing Tobit, Raphael also heals Sarah of her demon and Tobias of his fear of taking Sarah as his wife. This is why, writes Gregory, Raphael is called "God's remedy."

Even the fictitious name Raphael assumes when he is with Tobit and Tobias, namely, "Azariah, the son of the great Hananiah" (Tobit 5:13), indicates God's healing touch. *Azariah* means "Yahweh has helped," and *Hananiah* means "Yahweh is merciful."

Tobit's blindness and his restored sight are both attributed to God, even though Raphael's treatment—applying fish's gall to the white films (most likely cataracts)—reflects the medical practice of the time. Suffering is often seen as punishment for sin, and it is accepted as part of God's plan. As Raphael makes clear, however, all blessing also is due to God. Tobias is the instrument of God's providence, while Raphael is the messenger. But it is God who heals and who is to receive all praise.

Raphael's self-revelation as one of the seven angels who stands before God's glory is echoed by the author of the Book of Revelation, who refers to "seven flaming torches, which are the seven spirits of God" (Revelation 4:5) in front of the throne and "the seven angels who stand before God" (Revelation 8:2).

Raguel, Sarah's father, whose name means "friend of God," reminds us of Abraham, another friend of God who entertained angels without knowing it. In return Abraham received a son, while Raguel received a healed daughter and a son-in-law. The Book of Tobit says little else about Raguel. He merely joins the ranks of the others, namely Tobit and Tobias, who entertained the archangel Raphael without knowing it.

God continues to heal today. Raphael may appear in the person of a doctor who administers a drug or treatment that removes all traces of a disease. God's healing may come through the words of a counselor who listens intently and then guides a person to a more constructive lifestyle and greater mental stability. Sometimes the messenger of healing reveals his presence in the flash of an idea for relieving pain or for casting out the demon of despair. As long as we, like Raguel, remain open to entertaining angels, we can know that in moments of distress or blindness or pain God will send his angel-messenger to heal us.

Like Tobit, Tobias, and Raguel, we usually entertain angels without being aware that we have done so. We know Raphael has been with us only by the healing he leaves behind.

MEDITATION

> In what way has God healed you?

> Have you been healed of emotional or spiritual pain?

> Have you ever had a physical cure?

> Who was the "archangel" who was God's instrument of your cure?

PRAYER

Blessed be God,

    and blessed be his great name,

    and blessed be all his holy angels.

May his holy name be blessed

    throughout all the ages.

Though he afflicted me,

he has had mercy upon me.

   . . . I exalt my God,

    and my soul rejoices in the King of heaven.

Let all people speak of his majesty,

    and acknowledge him in Jerusalem.

Tobit 11:14-15; 13:7-8

Three Angels

for

OCTOBER

God Guards

God Reveals Dependence

Christ Deserves Worship

God Guards

The LORD said to Moses, "... I am going to send an angel in front of you, to guard you on the way and to bring you to the place that I have prepared. Be attentive to him and listen to his voice; do not rebel against him, for he will not pardon your transgression; for my name is in him. But if you listen attentively to his voice and do all that I say, then I will be an enemy to your enemies and a foe to your foes .... My angel goes in front of you."

Exodus 20:22; 23:20-23

REFLECTION

On October 2, the Roman Catholic Church celebrates the Memorial of the Guardian Angels. At one time the popular focus of the commemoration was the understanding that God provides for each person a guardian angel, who accompanies him or her through life from the cradle to the grave. The "Angel of God" prayer, learned by many Catholics who attended parochial schools, developed from that view of guardian angels:

Angel of God, my guardian dear,

to whom his love commits me here,

ever this day be at my side,

to light and guard, to rule and guide.

Amen.

The prayers assigned for the Mass on October 2 indicate today's focus of this feast—namely, that God guards and protects people. The Opening Prayer focuses on God's providence:

God our Father,

in your loving providence

you send your holy angels to watch over us.

Hear our prayers,

defend us always by their protection

and let us share your life with them for ever.

The memorial is solidly based on a biblical understanding of God's care. God will be with his people; his angel will bring them to the promised land. The people are to obey the angel, who is God in disguise.

The Bible pictures the divine presence in various ways: the angel who travels in front of the Israelites (see Exodus 32:34; 33:2); the pillars of cloud and fire (see Exodus 13:21; 40:36-38); the ark of the covenant (see Numbers 10:33). Some of the Fathers of the Church were particularly interested in the concept of God as guardian angel.

The Shepherd of Hermas, an anonymous work written between 140 and 155 CE, says that after God created people, he gave them to the Son, who appointed the angels to guard them. Late in the second century, St. Clement of Alexandria speculated that regiments of angels are assigned to nations, cities, and perhaps individuals. In the fourth century, St. Basil the Great understood angels to be guardians both of nations and of individuals. Origen, a third-century Alexandrian theologian, gave us the concept of two angels—one good and one bad—guiding people.

From the eighth century, emphasis increased on personal guardian angels. Not just every baptized person, but *every* human being was thought to have his or her own guardian angel from birth. The catechism of the sixteenth-century Council of Trent taught that God placed people under the protection of guardian angels as part of his fatherly care.

Today's *Catechism of the Catholic Church* also mentions the protective role of guardian angels. It says that from infancy to death, human life is surrounded by the angels' watchfulness and intercession. Theologian Karl Rahner has said that no objection can be raised to the concept of guardian angels, providing they are not pictured too anthropomorphically or childishly.

Put simply, the guardian angel is God's help, which is near at hand. God guards and cares for us, even though most of the time we are unaware of this divine protection.

A child falls into an old well and is missing for days. When she is found, she has not a single scratch. God has been busy guarding the child.

A woman walks home alone through the park after dark. She hears heavy footsteps getting closer and closer. Suddenly she comes upon a couple sitting on a bench, and they agree to accompany her to a well-lighted street. Through the couple, God is guarding the woman.

God's help is not always so dramatic, of course. If we fail to recognize his presence, it may be because God is protecting us from evil and danger even before we have the chance to get frightened. Whenever we do discover that God has protected us, we can be sure of something else: We have entertained one of his angel-messengers.

(ɔeɖitation

> When has God guarded you?

> From what or whom were you protected?

> Who was the "angel" who represented God's presence to you?

prayer

My help comes from the LORD,

who made heaven and earth.

He will not let your foot be moved;

he who keeps you will not slumber.

He who keeps Israel

will neither slumber nor sleep.

The LORD is your keeper;

the LORD is your shade at your right hand.

The LORD will keep you from all evil;

he will keep your life.

The LORD will keep

your going out and your coming in

from this time on and forevermore.

Psalm 121:2-5, 7-8

God Reveals Dependence

SCRIPTURE

The disciples came to Jesus and asked, "Who is the greatest in the kingdom of heaven?" He called a child, whom he put among them, and said, "Truly I tell you, unless you change and become like children, you will never enter the kingdom of heaven. Whoever becomes humble like this child is the greatest in the kingdom of heaven. Whoever welcomes one such child in my name welcomes me. Take care that you do not despise one of these little ones; for, I tell you, in heaven their angels continually see the face of my Father in heaven."

Matthew 18:1-5, 10

REFLECTION

We spend our first twenty or twenty-five years becoming adults—often not quickly enough to suit our parents, who may wail in despair, "When are you going to grow up?" Then we spend our next forty to fifty years learning the meaning of adulthood. Somewhere around the age of seventy or eighty, we begin relearning how to be children.

Adulthood means independence: responsibility for oneself, the ability to do as one pleases. Childhood, whether that of youth or that of old age, means dependence: reliance on someone else to fulfill basic needs, submission to those who provide care. The independent adult is in every way superior to the dependent child. This, at least, is the usual Western view of adulthood and childhood. The author of Matthew's Gospel, however, sees life from a different perspective.

Who is the greatest in the kingdom of heaven? Whoever becomes humble like a child. In the ancient world a child had no rights at all. He or she was considered the property of his or her father until the daughter matured and was handed over to another father seeking a wife for a son, or until the son came of age and began learning his father's trade in preparation to inherit the older man's business and estate. If a father didn't want a child, he could

125

expose it, have it aborted, or kill it at birth. If a father was angry at his child, he could beat it or kill it.

The child is a sign of humility, not because children are naturally humble (they aren't!) but because they are dependent. To humble oneself is to limit oneself just as Jesus did:

[He] emptied himself

taking the form of a slave,

being born in human likeness.

And being found in human form,

he humbled himself

and became obedient to the point of death—

even death on a cross (Philippians 2:7-8).

For Matthew's audience, the "little ones" are the minor members of the community: the marginalized, the people with no power of their own. For people in positions of power, Jesus has a warning. Do not be arrogant, he says. These little ones have powerful connections. Angels link them directly with their Father in heaven!

Where the Book of Daniel speaks of angels assigned to guard nations (see Daniel 10:13, 20-21), Matthew's Gospel individualizes angelic care. The evangelist transforms the concept of God's protection of Israel into that of God's protection of every human being. The weaker the human, the more powerful his or her protector. The guardian angels of the "little ones" see the face of God, whom they serve.

If independent, authoritarian adults humble themselves and become like children, they too will be guarded by heavenly beings who look upon God's face. Humility is not gained overnight, however; it comes after a lifetime of slow transformation into total dependence upon God.

OEDITATION

- ➢ When do you act like an independent adult?
- ➢ When do you act like a dependent child?
- ➢ In which instance do you entertain "angels"?

PRAYER

You who live in the shelter of the Most High,

> who abide in the shadow of the Almighty,

> will say to the LORD, "My refuge and my fortress;

> my God, in whom I trust."

. . . He will cover you with his pinions,

> and under his wings you will find refuge . . . .

Because you have made the LORD your refuge,

> the Most High your dwelling place,

> no evil shall befall you,

> nor scourge come near your tent,

For he will command his angels concerning you,

> to guard you in all your ways.

On their hands they will bear you up,

> so that you will not dash your foot against a stone.

Psalm 91:1-2, 4, 9-12

Christst Deserves Worship

SCRIPTURE

Then I saw in the right hand of the one seated on the throne a scroll written on the inside and on the back, sealed with seven seals; and I saw a mighty angel proclaiming with a loud voice, "Who is worthy to open the scroll and break its seals?" And no one in heaven or on earth or under the earth was able to open the scroll or to look into it. And I began to weep bitterly because no one was found worthy to open the scroll or to look into it.

Then one of the elders said to me, "Do not weep. See, the Lion of the tribe of Judah, the Root of David, has conquered, so that he can open the scroll and its seven seals."

Then I saw between the throne and the four living creatures and among the elders a Lamb standing as if it had been slaughtered, having seven horns and seven eyes, which are the seven spirits of God sent out into all the earth. He went and took the scroll from the right hand of the one who was seated on the throne. When he had taken the scroll, the four living creatures and the twenty-four elders fell before the Lamb, each holding a harp and golden bowls full of incense, which are the prayers of the saints. They sing a new song:

"You are worthy to take the scroll

and open its seals,

for you were slaughtered and by your blood

you ransomed for God

saints from every tribe and language

and people and nation;

you have made them to be a kingdom and priests

serving our God,

and they will reign on earth."

Then I looked, and I heard the voice of many angels surrounding the throne and the living creatures and the elders; they numbered myriads of myriads and thousands of thousands, singing with full voice,

"Worthy is the Lamb that was slaughtered

to receive power and wealth and wisdom and might

and honor and glory and blessing!"

Then I heard every creature in heaven and on earth and under the earth and in the sea, and all that is in them, singing,

"To the one seated on the throne and to the Lamb

be blessing and honor and glory and might

forever and ever!"

And the four living creatures said, "Amen!" And the elders fell down and worshiped.

Revelation 5:1-14

REFLECTION

When we hear the word *lamb*, we think of newness, gentleness, weakness, innocence. We picture the clumsy newborn sheep trying to stand on its shaky legs as it searches for its mother's teat and nuzzles close to suck warm milk. So we are startled when we read in the Book of Revelation about the slaughtered Lamb with seven horns and seven eyes. Who is this bizarre creature?

Surprisingly, it is Christ. Like any lamb, he demonstrates newness, gentleness, weakness, and innocence. Yet, like the Passover lamb of Exodus 12 whose blood saves the firstborn of Egypt and Israel, or the silent, doomed lamb of Isaiah 53 who carries "the iniquity of us all" (Isaiah 53:6), this Lamb also suffers and dies. He is an image of Christ, the Paschal Lamb, the innocent one who died on the cross and was raised by God for the salvation of all.

This Christ-Lamb is no ordinary farm animal. He has seven horns, representing complete power, and seven eyes, indicating perfect knowledge. He is the "Lion of the tribe of Judah" and the "Root of David" (Revelation 5:5)—in other words, the fulfillment of the Davidic dynasty, the long-awaited Messiah.

The Lamb is the magnificent new king who has triumphed, not by avoiding suffering and death but by immersing himself in them and being raised from the dead by God's Spirit.

Therefore only the Lamb is worthy to open the scroll in which end-time events are recorded. Only the Lamb can initiate these events, through which God will triumph. Only the Lamb is worthy of worship by innumerable living creatures and elders and angels.

This picture of heavenly worship parallels the way Roman emperors were acclaimed. Because of the Lamb's sacrifice, however, honor is given to the Lamb rather than to any human powers. As we gather around the Lamb's throne, the voices of countless angels lead us in our praise.

MEDITATION

➢ What does the slaughtered Lamb have to do with your past, present, and future?

➢ When have you experienced the union of the past, present, and future while worshiping God in and through Christ?

➢ Who was the "angel" you entertained?

PRAYER

Praise the LORD!

Praise the LORD from the heavens;

    praise him in the heights!

Praise him, all his angels;

    praise him, all his host!

Praise him, sun and moon;

    praise him, all you shining stars!

Praise him, you highest heavens,

    and you waters above the heavens!

Let them praise the name of the LORD,

for he commanded and they were created.

He established them forever and ever;

he fixed their bounds, which cannot be passed.

Psalm 148:1-6

ThREE ANGELS

fOR

NOVEMBER

God Controls

God Speaks

God Sees

God Controls

[The Son] is the image of the invisible God, the firstborn of all creation; for in him all things in heaven and on earth were created, things visible and the invisible, whether thrones or dominions or rulers or powers—all things have been created through him and for him. He himself is before all things, and in him all things hold together. He is the head of the body, the church; he is the beginning, the firstborn from the dead, so that he might come to have first place in everything. For in him all the fullness of God was pleased to dwell, and through him God was pleased to reconcile to himself all things, whether on earth or in heaven, by making peace through the blood of his cross.

Colossians 1:15-20

REFLECTION

The theme of this ancient hymn is Christ's role in creation. Through Christ, God created everything that exists. Therefore all creation is subject to Christ and consequently to God.

Christ created and rules "all things in heaven" as well as on earth. The hymn lists four categories of angelic beings—thrones, dominions, rulers, and powers—all subordinate to Christ. In Colossae, where angel worship was popular, these beings may have been seen as rivals of Christ. It is clear from other New Testament passages that at least some of these angels are hostile, even though they are God's creation.

In the New Testament, only this selection from Colossians includes *thrones* as a category of angel. *Dominions* as an angelic category occurs only here and in the Letter to the Ephesians (1:21), where God's might is revealed in Christ's resurrection and ascension and in his exaltation over all angelic forces.

Rulers and *powers*, or *authorities*, usually mentioned together, are found twice more in Colossians. In chapter 2, verse 10, Christ is called "the head of every ruler and authority;" in verse 15, Christ, like a triumphant Roman emperor, is said to have "disarmed the rulers and authorities."

The Letter to the Ephesians mentions rulers and powers three times. First, Christ is seated at God's right hand, "far above all rule and authority and power and dominion" (Ephesians 1:21). Second, God makes his wisdom known through the Church to "rulers and authorities in the heavenly places" (Ephesians 3:10). Third, the Christian life is a constant struggle against malevolent "rulers, against the authorities, against the cosmic powers of this present darkness, against the spiritual forces of evil in the heavenly places" (Ephesians 6:12).

St. Paul, in the Letter to the Romans, mentions rulers along with powers and angels: ". . . I am convinced that neither death, nor life, nor angels, nor rulers, nor things present, nor things to come, nor powers, nor height, nor depth, nor anything else in all creation, will be able to separate us from the love of God in Christ Jesus our Lord" (Romans 8:38-39). In his First Letter to the Corinthians, Paul writes that Christ will destroy "every ruler and every authority and power" (1 Corinthians 15:24).

The author of the First Letter of Peter likewise says that "angels, authorities, and powers" have been subjected to Christ (1 Peter 3:22).

From this survey of thrones, dominions, rulers, powers, and authorities we can see two biblical themes. First, all angelic beings, whether friendly or unfriendly, were created by God in Christ. Second, all heavenly beings, whether helpful or hostile, are subject to Christ. God is in complete control.

In our age of technology and information, we humans often act as though we believe we determine both life and death. We need to realize that God alone creates life through Christ, who has conquered death for us and offers us eternal life.

Whenever we squeeze God out of our decision-making process and begin to think we are in control, we need to be forcefully reminded that God is superior. If even angels—friendly or unfriendly—are subject to his will, how can we think we are in charge?

MEDITATION

> When have you most recently been reminded that God is in control of all that exists?

> Who was the "angel" who reminded you?

PRAYER

O LORD, our Sovereign,

> how majestic is your name in all the earth!

When I look at your heavens, the work of your fingers,

> the moon and the stars that you have established;

what are human beings that you are mindful of them,

> mortals that you care for them?

Yet you have made them a little lower than God,

> and crowned them with glory and honor.

You have given them dominion over the works of your hands;

> you have put all things under their feet . . . .

O LORD, our Sovereign,

> how majestic is your name in all the earth!

Psalm 8:1, 3-6, 9

God Speaks

SCRIPTURE

And I saw another mighty angel coming down from heaven, wrapped in a cloud, with a rainbow over his head; his face was like the sun, and his legs like pillars of fire. He held a little scroll open in his hand. Setting his right foot on the sea and his left foot on the land, he gave a great shout, like a lion roaring. Then the voice that I had heard from heaven spoke to me again, saying, "Go, take the scroll that is open in the hand of the angel who is standing on the sea and on the land." So I went to the angel and told him to give me the little scroll; and he said to me, "Take it, and eat; it will be bitter to your stomach, but sweet as honey in your mouth." So I took the little scroll from the hand of the angel and ate it; it was sweet as honey in my mouth, but when I had eaten it, my stomach was made bitter.

Then they said to me, "You must prophesy again about many peoples and nations and languages and kings."

Revelation 10:1-3a, 8-11

REFLECTION

John the Revelator is still in vision. What he sees is dramatic, colorful, and strange, rich in symbol and metaphor. John—and the Christian Church for millennia to come—will have to ponder the spectacle in order to understand it.

The first thing John sees is "another mighty angel," who holds an open scroll. John takes the scroll and eats it. It is sweet to the taste, but it leaves him with indigestion. What is going on here?

Many of John's early readers would have found this incident familiar. It would have reminded them of a similar scene from the Book of Ezekiel, who records his vision this way:

I heard the voice of someone speaking . . . . He said to me, Mortal, I am sending you to the people of Israel, to a nation of rebels who have rebelled against me . . . . But you, mortal, hear what I say to you: do not be rebellious like that rebellious house;

open your mouth and eat what I give you.

I looked, and a hand was stretched out to me, and a written scroll was in it . . . .

He said to me: O mortal, eat what is offered to you; eat this scroll, and go, speak to the house of Israel. So I opened my mouth, and he gave me the scroll to eat. He said to me, Mortal, eat this scroll that I give you and fill your stomach with it. Then I ate it; and in my mouth it was as sweet as honey.

He said to me: Mortal, go to the house of Israel and speak my very words to them.

Ezekiel 1:28-2:3, 8-9; 3:1-4

John, like Ezekiel, is being commissioned to prophesy. By taking the scroll, both prophets signify that they are accepting their mission from God. By eating it, they make God's word part of their flesh. They are then sent to proclaim God's incarnate word.

At first both prophets find the word sweet: They know that God's people will be victorious. But then Ezekiel goes out to preach to people who do not want to listen to him, and John finds the word turning sour in his stomach.

How often God's word, when we first hear it, brings us peace and joy! But then we experience the pain and struggle involved in living what we hear. As John discovered, hearing God's word can be both sweet and bitter.

John the Revelator sees the angel standing with one foot on the land and one foot on the sea, a sign that God's message is for the entire earth. The open scroll represents the second cycle of visions in the Book of Revelation, which depict the end-time conflict between good and evil. John, like Ezekiel, is sent out to prophesy—not only to the people of Israel, but to the whole world. His message—that good has triumphed over evil—is for us.

God's angel with the scroll comes to us in many forms: books, magazines, newspapers, even E-mail. When we digest the spiritual truths we discover in our reading, we permit God's word to get inside us and transform us. Our best source of nourishment, of course, is the Bible. Spending a few minutes with a scriptural passage every day provides food for thought. It enables God to speak to us and to send us out to prophesy—that is, to speak God's words to others.

Our task, like that of Ezekiel and John the Revelator, is to entertain the angel of the scroll and receive the heavenly message, which is simultaneously sweet and sour.

Meditation

> When have you found the word of God simultaneously sweet and sour?

> What was its sweetness?

> What was its sourness?

> Who was the "angel" who fed you?

Prayer

The heavens are telling the glory of God;

and the firmament proclaims his handiwork.

Day to day pours forth speech,

and night to night declares knowledge.

There is no speech, nor are there words;

their voice is not heard;

yet their voice goes out through all the earth,

and their words to the end of the world.

The law of the LORD is perfect,

reviving the soul;

the decrees of the LORD are sure,

making wise the simple;

the precepts of the LORD are right,

rejoicing the heart;

the commandment of the LORD is clear,

enlightening the eyes;

the fear of the LORD is pure,

enduring forever;

the ordinances of the LORD are true

    and righteous altogether.

More to be desired are they than gold,

    even much fine gold;

sweeter also than honey,

    and drippings of the honeycomb.

Let the words of my mouth and the meditation of my heart

    be acceptable to you,

O LORD, my rock and my redeemer.

Psalm 19:1-4, 7-10, 14

God Sees

SCRIPTURE

Blessed be the God and Father of our Lord Jesus Christ! By his great mercy he has given us a new birth into a living hope through the resurrection of Jesus Christ from the dead, and into an inheritance that is imperishable, undefiled, and unfading, kept in heaven for you, who are being protected by the power of God through faith for a salvation ready to be revealed in the last time. In this you rejoice, even if now for a little while you have had to suffer various trials, so that the genuineness of your faith—being more precious than gold that, though perishable, is tested by fire—may be found to result in praise and glory and honor when Jesus Christ is revealed. Although you have not seen him, you love him; and even though you do not see him now, you believe in him and rejoice with an indescribable and glorious joy, for you are receiving the outcome of your faith, the salvation of your souls.

Concerning this salvation, the prophets who prophesied of the grace that was to be yours made careful search and inquiry, inquiring about the person or time that the Spirit of Christ within them indicated when it testified in advance to the sufferings destined for Christ and the subsequent glory. It was revealed to them that they were serving not themselves but you, in regard to the things that have now been announced to you through those who brought you good news by the Holy Spirit sent from heaven—things into which angels long to look!

1 Peter 1:3-12

REFLECTION

We begin every day of our lives by opening our eyes, and we end every day by closing them. In between the time of their opening and closing, we see people and things, read facial expressions and newspapers, determine safe passing distances and find our way around. Only by closing our eyes and imagining living a whole day without sight could we even begin to understand the importance of the gift of sight. And yet we see some of life's most important truths by faith, not with our eyes.

God, who is pure Spirit, does not have eyes. Yet we often speak of his "seeing" us. Since angels are God's messengers, we can also speak of them as if they can see. The author of the First Letter of Peter does this when he writes that "angels long to look" into God's plan of salvation. The image is that of peeking through a window.

What is it angels want to see as they peer through the glass? The one-word answer in 1 Peter is *hope*. Hope enables a person to keep on going, confident that God will provide salvation. Hope is imperishable.

Hope persists even through hardship and persecution, says the author of this letter. That is because Jesus Christ is coming again to reveal his salvation to the whole universe. By "seeing" this hope, and by knowing that persecution is one way to share Christ's passion, Christians can hold on to their faith.

Thanks to the revelation of God in Christ, we can "see" hope today; we can stand next to the angels gazing through the window and get a glimpse of God's plan.

Parents, for example, see hope in their son or daughter who graduates from college. The cap and gown, the processional, and the diploma are visual signs of hope for a successful life, a good job, security, a spouse and children, the ability to make a difference in the world. For a fleeting moment parents see what all the study, struggle, and cost has earned. However, they don't get to look through the window very long. Life moves on quickly, and angel-messengers don't stay around once hope is glimpsed.

Maybe you've seen hope etched on the face of a person suffering from an incurable disease. Surprisingly often, hospitals and nursing facilities and hospices are filled with hope. The calmness with which a person speaks about his or her illness, the lack of regret or anger, and the serenity that fills the room can be a vision of hope to others. In this situation, you somehow know that you have just entertained an angel peeking through the window at your side.

God is always leading us to the windows where we can see hope. The curtains may part while we are watching the sunrise over the ocean, reading a good book, or being boisterous with family and friends. Wherever and whenever we see hope, we know that we have been blessed. God has sent an angel-messenger of hope to permit us to see, for a moment, that for which our hearts greatly yearn.

MEDITATION

> ➤ When have you most recently "seen" hope?

> ➤ How was it revealed to you?

> ➤ Who was the "angel" of hope you entertained?

PRAYER

For God alone my soul waits in silence;
    from him comes my salvation.
He alone is my rock and my salvation,
    my fortress; I shall never be shaken.
For God alone my soul waits in silence,
    for my hope is from him.
He alone is my rock and my salvation,
    my fortress; I shall not be shaken.
On God rests my deliverance and my honor,
    my mighty rock, my refuge is in God.
Trust in him at all times, O people;
    pour out your heart before him;
God is a refuge for us.

Psalm 62:1-2, 5-8

THREE ANGELS

FOR

DECEMBER

God Inspires Dreams

God Brings Good News

God Owns the Future

God Inspires Dreams

SCRIPTURE

Now the birth of Jesus the Messiah took place in this way. When his mother Mary had been engaged to Joseph, but before they lived together, she was found to be with child from the Holy Spirit. Her husband Joseph, being a righteous man and unwilling to expose her to public disgrace, planned to dismiss her quietly. But just when he had resolved to do this, an angel of the Lord appeared to him in a dream and said, "Joseph, son of David, do not be afraid to take Mary as your wife, for the child conceived in her is from the Holy Spirit. She will bear a son, and you are to name him Jesus, for he will save his people from their sins."

. . . An angel of the Lord appeared to Joseph in a dream and said, "Get up, take the child and his mother, and flee to Egypt, and remain there until I tell you; for Herod is about to search for the child, to destroy him." Then Joseph got up, took the child and his mother by night, and went to Egypt . . . .

. . . An angel of the Lord suddenly appeared in a dream to Joseph in Egypt and said, "Get up, take the child and his mother, and go to the land of Israel, for those who were seeking the child's life are dead." Then Joseph got up, took the child and his mother, and went to the land of Israel.

Matthew 1:18-21; 2:13-14, 19-21

REFLECTION

In the account of Jesus' birth in the Gospel of Matthew, an angel of the Lord repeatedly plays a major role. The messenger, who prefers to appear in dreams, tells Joseph to marry his fiancée, to flee to Egypt, and to return to Israel.

Matthew's account clearly shows that Jesus' story is a continuation, a fulfillment, of Israel's story. It does this by frequent allusions to the Hebrew Scriptures known by Joseph, by Matthew, and by Matthew's readers.

The angel of the Lord reminds us of the angel who appeared to Abraham, to Moses, to Gideon, and to Manoah's wife, among others, signaling divine intervention and revealing God's presence among his people.

Joseph's dreams call to mind the dreams of another Joseph, a son of Jacob the patriarch and eventually the ruler of all Egypt.

The trip into and out of Egypt alludes to Israel's escape to that land during a time of famine and its exodus several generations later.

The name *Jesus*, "Yahweh saves," is another form of the name *Joshua*, the fearless leader who brought Israel into the promised land after Moses' death. In Jesus as in Joshua, God is at work helping and saving people.

When Joseph entertained an angel in his dreams, he listened carefully to what the angel said and then immediately acted on the message. Angel-messengers continue to visit us in our dreams today. Like Joseph, we can welcome them, listen to them, and act. If we are looking for a long-skirted person with wings and a halo, however, we may miss the revelation that God wants to share with us through our dreams.

Often we go to bed with an unsolved problem on our minds. During the night, an angel of the Lord may work through our unconscious to bring forth the very solution that God has conceived for us through the Spirit. Behold, just as we step out of bed the next morning, the solution hits us and we know what action to take.

Dreams can reveal our unknown fears to us. Fear is a handicap; it keeps us from living abundantly. If we do not turn away the angel of the Lord, we may discover that God has revealed to us one of our fears through our dreams. Behold, once we can name the fear, we can proceed to deal with it so that it no longer harms us.

God may also reveal himself to us through daydreams. By imagining ourselves as we would like to be, we take the first step on the path of conversion. Behold, our daydream becomes an invitation for the angel of the Lord to direct us to the road that God wants us to travel.

God reveals himself in dreams to people in all ages—not only to Joseph, son of Jacob, and to Joseph, husband of Mary, but also to you and to me.

MEDITATION

> ➤ When have you received an insight, found a solution to a problem, or become aware of one of your hidden fears in a dream?

> ➤ Who was the "angel" you entertained?

PRAYER

O give thanks to the LORD, call on his name,

    make known his deeds among the peoples.

Sing to him, sing praises to him;

    tell of all his wonderful works.

Glory in his holy name;

    let the hearts of those who seek the LORD rejoice.

Seek the LORD and his strength;

    seek his presence continually.

Remember the wonderful works he has done,

    his miracles, and the judgments he uttered . . . .

When he summoned famine against the land,

    and broke every staff of bread,

    he had sent a man ahead of them,

    Joseph, who was sold as a slave.

Then Israel came to Egypt;

    Jacob lived as an alien in the land of Ham.

And the LORD made his people very fruitful,

    and made them stronger than their foes . . . .

He sent his servant Moses,

    and Aaron whom he had chosen.

So he brought his people out with joy,

    his chosen ones with singing.

Psalm 105:1-5, 16-17, 23-24, 26, 43

God Brings Good News

SCRIPTURE

There were shepherds living in the fields, keeping watch over their flock by night. Then an angel of the Lord stood before them, and the glory of the Lord shone around them, and they were terrified. But the angel said to them, "Do not be afraid; for see—I am bringing you good news of great joy for all the people: to you is born this day in the city of David a Savior, who is the Messiah, the Lord. This will be a sign for you: you will find a child wrapped in bands of cloth and lying in a manger."

And suddenly there was with the angel a multitude of the heavenly host, praising God and saying,

"Glory to God in the highest heaven,

and on earth peace among those whom he favors!"

When the angels had left them and gone into heaven, the shepherds said to one another, "Let us go now to Bethlehem and see this thing that has taken place, which the Lord has made known to us." So they went with haste and found Mary and Joseph, and the child lying in the manger. When they saw this, they made known what had been told them about this child; and all who heard it were amazed at what the shepherds told them. But Mary treasured all these words and pondered them in her heart. The shepherds returned, glorifying and praising God for all they had heard and seen, as it had been told them.

Luke 2:8-20

REFLECTION

The angels' song of praise at Christ's birth continues to resound in the Church's hymn of praise, the *Gloria*: "Glory to God in the highest!"

It is no accident that the good news came first to shepherds. David, the great king of Israel, was himself a shepherd, and the newborn King was to be David's successor. Furthermore, shepherds—in those days considered people of very low status, even outlaws in some cases—reinforce Luke's theme of Jesus' ministry to the outcast. The angels, like Jesus, came to bring God's good news to the poor, the captives, the oppressed (see Luke 4:17-21).

What is the good news? The Messiah has been born! Not King Herod, not Caesar Augustus, not a powerful human general, but a baby in a feeding trough, who will save Israel and the whole world.

Suddenly we know what we have suspected when, at the beginning of the account, Luke told us that "the glory of the Lord shone around." This scene is a theophany, a revelation of God. As soon as the lone divine messenger has announced the good news, the scene erupts with all the spirits who dwell in God's presence. The shepherds see a "multitude of the heavenly host," perhaps the very ones who surround God's throne in the visions of Daniel and Revelation, shouting praises to God.

Once this heavenly chorus completes its hymn of praise and disappears, the shepherds go to Bethlehem, where they find the child just as the angel said. They then rush through the sleepy town, telling all they meet what they have seen and heard. Only then do they return to their flock, glorifying and praising God just as the heavenly beings had done. Now God is praised on earth as he is praised in heaven.

A four-part pattern emerges in Luke's story: The shepherds hear, they see, they proclaim, and they praise—all in response to God's good news. God continues to send us the same good news today, and we can respond as the shepherds did.

For example, after hearing a doctor's report that a biopsy sample is not malignant, we see how God cares for us, we tell others, and we say a prayer of thanksgiving.

We hear God's good news in the birth of a healthy child, whose parents see the miracle, rush to share their delight with the rest of their family, and praise God for the marvel they have witnessed.

Every time we receive good news, we can be sure an angel-messenger is nearby. It is God who brings good news into our lives. Once we hear it, we see what God is doing and proclaim it to others, all the while thanking God for the privilege of receiving his revelation.

MEDITATION

> ➤ When have you most recently received some good news?

> ➤ What did you see or understand about it?

> ➤ Whom did you tell?

> ➤ In what ways did you praise or thank God?

> ➤ Who was the "angel" you entertained?

PRAYER

Rejoice in the LORD, O you righteous.

> Praise befits the upright.

Praise the LORD with the lyre;

> make melody to him with the harp of ten strings.

Sing to him a new song;

> play skillfully on the strings, with loud shouts.

By the word of the LORD the heavens were made;

> and all of their host by the breath of his mouth.

The LORD looks down from heaven;

> he sees all humankind.

From where he sits enthroned he watches

> all the inhabitants of the earth—

he who fashions the hearts of them all,

> and observes all their deeds.

Let your steadfast love, O LORD, be upon us,

> even as we hope in you.

Psalm 33:1-3, 6, 13-15, 22

God Owns the Future

[Jesus said to his disciples,] "The sign of the Son of Man will appear in heaven, and then all the tribes of the earth will mourn, and they will see 'the Son of Man coming on the clouds of heaven' with power and great glory. And he will send out his angels with a loud trumpet call, and they will gather his elect from the four winds, from one end of heaven to the other.

"From the fig tree learn its lesson: as soon as its branch becomes tender and puts forth its leaves, you know that summer is near. So also, when you see all these things, you know that he is near, at the very gates . . . .

"But about that day and hour no one knows, neither the angels of heaven, nor the Son, but only the Father."

Matthew 24:30-33, 36

REFLECTION

The author of Matthew's Gospel obviously loved the Hebrew Scriptures. When he wrote about Jesus' birth, he related contemporary events to well-known Bible stories. Here, writing about Jesus' second coming, he alludes to Daniel's vision of the Son of Man (see Daniel 7:13-14) and to Zechariah's prophecy about the mourning of the tribes of Earth (see Zechariah 12:10).

Likewise, the angels gathering the elect have an echo in the Old Testament. In the Book of Deuteronomy, Moses says to the Hebrews: "Even if you are exiled to the ends of the world, from there the LORD your God will gather you, and from there he will bring you back" (Deuteronomy 30:4). It is important to note that it is *God* who gathers the people.

Matthew has already used the image of gathering in the parable of the weeds among the wheat. In this story Jesus says that the weeds, representing the children of the evil one, and the wheat, representing the children of the kingdom, should grow together until the harvest. "The harvest is the end of the age," he says, "and the reapers are angels" (Matthew 13:39). When the time is ripe, the angels will separate the weeds from the wheat, the sinners from the saints. The kingdom, then, is a mix of saints and sinners until the final sifting by God's angel-messengers.

As Matthew begins his narrative about the final harvest of God's people and the judgment of the nations (see 25:31-46), he again mentions the Son of Man coming in glory "and all the angels with him." Earlier in the Gospel, Matthew has prepared the reader for this scene. In Jesus' words, "The Son of Man is to come with his angels in the glory of his Father, and then he will repay everyone for what has been done" (Matthew 16:27).

Matthew's message is clear: The end of the age is coming. Jesus will judge his kingdom, and angels will gather God's people in. But when will this happen?

Maybe soon. Maybe not for a long time. Jesus' parable of the fig tree (see 24:32-34) whose leaves announce the coming of summer stresses the imminence of the final judgment. On the other hand, Jesus' insistence that no one—not the Son, not the angels—knows when the end will come opens up the possibility of delay.

God is past, present, and future. All time belongs to God. Indeed, all time is in God, because the eternal God is not limited by time as we are. Why are angels involved in the second coming and gathering the elect and passing judgment? Because they, like we, live in this present in-between time, even as they—in a way we cannot imagine—also live in God's eternal present, which includes past and future.

From our limited perspective, all we can say is that the future belongs to God, and that our path toward God is lined with angels.

MEDITATION

> In what ways have you experienced the nearness of God's judgment?

> In what ways have you experienced its delay?

> What "angels" are leading you into the future?

PRAYER

O sing to the LORD a new song;

    sing to the LORD, all the earth.

Sing to the LORD, bless his name;

    tell of his salvation from day to day.

Declare his glory among the nations,

    his marvelous works among all peoples.

Let the heavens be glad, and let the earth rejoice;

    let the sea roar, and all that fills it;

    let the field exult, and everything in it.

Then shall all the trees of the forest sing for joy

    before the LORD; for he is coming,

    for he is coming to judge the earth.

He will judge the world with righteousness,

    and the peoples with his truth.

Psalm 96:1-3, 11-13

Index of Scripture Texts

The following Scripture texts are quoted in this book. They are listed by chapter and verse as they appear together on the pages listed.

About the Author

Father Mark G. Boyer, a priest of the Diocese of Springfield-Cape Girardeau, Missouri, is editor of his diocesan newspaper, *The Mirror*. He is also part-time instructor in biblical studies in the Religious Studies Department of Southwest Missouri State University, Springfield, Missouri.

In addition to numerous articles in a variety of periodicals, Father Boyer is the author of the following books:

Day by Day Through the Easter Season (Liguori)

Following the Star: Daily Reflections for Advent and Christmas (Liguori)

Mystagogy: Liturgical Paschal Spirituality for Lent and Easter (Alba House)

Return to the Lord: A Lenten Journey of Daily Reflections (Alba House)

The Liturgical Environment: What the Documents Say (The Liturgical Press)

Mary's Day—Saturday: Meditations for Marian Celebrations (The Liturgical Press)

Breathing Deeply of God's New Life: Preparing Spiritually for the Sacraments of Initiation (St. Anthony Messenger Press)

Why Suffer? The Answer of Jesus (The Pastoral Press)

Also Available from ACTA Publications

Here are more popular, biblically-based resources for personal enrichment or group use:

Life in Christ: Revised in Accordance with the New Catechism of the Catholic Church by Gerard Weber and James Killgallon. This catechism for adults in the traditional question-and-answer format has sold over two million copies. Explains the Catholic faith in a clear, concise and comprehensive matter, with extensive quotes from the Scriptures. 312 pages, $4.95

Life Transformed: Meditations on the Christian Scriptures in Light of Buddhist Perspectives by Leo Lefebure, with a Foreword by John Shea. Father Lefebure, a Christian theologian and a student of Buddhism, offers meditations on many of the most familiar texts from the Bible from the perspective of Buddhism. 186 pages, $9.95.

Gospel Spirituality: An Audio Retreat with John Shea. Master storyteller and theologian Father John Shea describes the center of the spirituality of the "Beloved Son of the Most High" who "came so that you might have life and have it more abundantly." Set of six 70-80 minute audio cassettes in vinyl album, $29.95.

Come and See: Living Lessons from the Gospel of John. Father John Shea offers new insight into three of the most popular stories from the Gospel of John: The Woman at the Well, The Man Born Blind, and The Raising of Lazarus. Included are dramatic interpretations of each story by Graziano and Nancy Marcheschi. Three 60-75 minute video tapes, $29.95 each or $69.95 for set.

The Daily Dilemma of the Christian: Philemon's Problem by James Burtchaell, CSC. A classic book on the dilemma posed by the Epistle to Philemon: Can one be both brother and master? Father Burtchaell analyzes the ethics of the Christian demanded by the Bible. 178 pages, $4.95.

'Shua by William Burke, with drawings by Mary Southard, CSJ. The fictional account of the life of Jesus as told by a childhood friend. Father William Burke uses his knowledge of Scripture and the times of Jesus to imagine what Jesus might have been like. 103 pages, $8.95.

Available from booksellers or call 800-397-2282